The Telegraphic Transmission of Photographs

THE TELEGRAPHIC TRANSMISSION OF PHOTOGRAPHS

A part of the *Daily Mirror* Installation, showing the Korn Telautograph (at back), and the Thorne-Baker Telectrograph. The operator (Mr. A. Tucker) is adjusting Prof. Korn's galvanometer.

[Frontispiece.

THE TELEGRAPHIC TRANSMISSION OF PHOTOGRAPHS

BY

T. THORNE BAKER,

F.C.S., F.R.P.S., A.I.E.E.

LONDON

CONSTABLE & COMPANY LIMITED

10 ORANGE STREET LEICESTER SQUARE W.C.

1910

PREFACE

VERY little is known at present about the telegraphy of pictures, because the published descriptions of the instruments in use have been confined almost entirely to technical journals. The desire to have news at the earliest possible moment, and the recent demand by the public to have the "news in pictures," has opened up the field for a new science, which is a peculiar mixture of electricity, optics and photo-engraving. The telegraphed picture, at first looked upon as a marvel, now occasions little or no surprise, which means that it is sufficiently like an ordinary photograph to pass muster among the other pictures in the newspaper in which it appears.

During the last two-and-a-half years, a great deal of experimental work has been carried out by me for *The Daily Mirror*, and it has been very largely owing to the active interest this journal has shown in photo-telegraphy that the pioneer work in this country has been possible. The interest displayed in the work by the editor, Mr. Alex. Kenealy, has never failed, and to his encouragement and enterprise the present position of this new branch of telegraphic work is largely due.

The descriptions given in the book of the systems in use to-day will, I hope, make quite clear to the reader "how it is done." Though certain portions of the matter are intended for those already conversant with the general principles of electricity, the bulk of the book has been written as simply as possible, and if the said portions are just passed over by the non-technical reader, I think the rest will be of interest to him.

At the time of going to press, preparations are being made for an endeavour to transmit photographs by wireless telegraphy across the Wash, the Postmaster-General having courteously allowed me the use of the experimental wireless stations at Hunstanton and Skegness. The last chapter, therefore, dealing with wireless work, will make the reader acquainted with the latest phase of photo-telegraphic work.

T. THORNE BAKER

15, Grosvenor Gardens,
    Cricklewood, N.W.,
        March, 1910.

CONTENTS

CONTENTS

LIST OF ILLUSTRATIONS

FULL PAGE ILLUSTRATIONS.

ILLUSTRATIONS IN TEXT.

THE TELEGRAPHIC
TRANSMISSION OF PHOTOGRAPHS

CHAPTER I.

ATTEMPTS AT THE SOLUTION OF THE TELE-GRAPHIC TRANSMISSION OF PHOTOGRAPHS AND PICTURES.

THE problem of transmitting a sketch or photograph over a distance by means of electricity has occupied the minds of many engineers and scientists for the past sixty years, but it has been up to the present time a singularly ungrateful task, owing to the lack of possible application. The tendency for modern journals to be illustrated with photographs has very greatly widened the scope for an instrument by which they can be " wired," and it is probably for this reason that so much attention has of late been devoted to this new science.

It seems difficult on first thought to conceive how a picture can be telegraphed. But a picture, just like a written message, can be split up into component parts ; the letters forming a word have a distinct meaning when seen assembled together in

P.T.   B

proper order, while the dots and dashes forming a
letter, according to the Morse code, possess similarly an intelligent meaning when grouped together
in correct order ; by building up a complete picture
with dots or small areas of varying depth, size,
or density we can produce a picture in a strictly
comparable manner.   One ingenious attempt at the
solution of photo-telegraphy—as ingenious as it is
impracticable—has been to divide up a picture into
thousands of small parts, representing each by a
certain letter of the alphabet, according to its density ; thus a light part might be called C or D, a
dark part Y or Z, and so on.   The letters are telegraphed to an operator, who forms a fresh picture
by building it up with small " parts," whose
densities are in accordance with the respective
letters.   Such a system is indeed possible, but would
require a very great amount of time.   It is the
minutes and seconds which have to be saved in
telegraphing a picture—especially in these days of
rapid railway transit, where photographic plates can
be sent to the newspaper office in a few hours,
so that only very late events are telegraphed.

This book is not intended to be historical, and I
shall therefore refer only to such early processes as
have a direct bearing upon the work that is being
done to-day.   Of early attempts at the transmission
of *pictures*, the Bakewell system deserves particular
notice, since upon it is based one of the three

most successful modern methods of transmission.
Bakewell's machine, which created some attention
as far back as 1847, consisted of two synchronously
revolving metal cylinders—one at each end of the
telegraph lines, over each of which a metal style
traced a spiral path (in the manner of the modern
phonograph). Upon one cylinder was placed a
sheet of tinfoil with the sketch drawn in ink made
with shellac, and on the receiving drum was placed
a sheet of paper prepared chemically, so that on

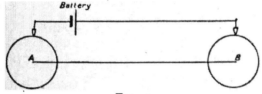

FIG. I.

passing an electric current through it a chemical
mark or stain was made. It appeared as seen in
Fig. I in its simplest form. A and B represent
the two cylinders, tracing over which are shown
two styles. A battery is in the circuit. It will
be readily seen that when a line in the sketch
which consists of shellac, comes under the style of
A, the current flowing through the circuit will be
broken, whereas when the bare tinfoil lies between
style and cylinder the current will flow.

This current therefore flows intermittently
through the chemically-prepared paper attached to
the drum *B*, and *when* it flows, it causes a chemical

mark on the paper. Hence, when the style has traced over the entire length of the sketch at A, the latter will be reproduced (negatively) at B. By suitable means it can, of course, be received positively if desired.

Such is the system which is now over sixty years old, and many trials were made with it to telegraph writing over distances ; here, however, the difficulties met with in long cables were at once felt ; attempts were actually made at one time in France to use such a system commercially, but they were soon abandoned.

Thence onwards continuous attempts were made to solve the problem of transmitting sketches, pictures, and photographs ; a long list of names of these early workers might be given. But we may well confine our attention at present to two men, Amstutz and Shelford Bidwell, as the ideas of these men were actually the germs of two important processes which have now given most satisfactory results. The latter made use of the newly discovered sensitiveness to light of the metal *selenium*, the former of the possibility to use the relief in a certain form of photographic image to vary the strength of the electric current.

On the lines followed by Bidwell, Ayrton and Perry also made experiments, both therefore utilising selenium at the sending station. Let us suppose that a portrait is to be telegraphed from this station to a distant receiving station. The portrait is projected on to a screen, where light and shade and varying tones are produced. Now suppose this screen divided up into a thousand square sections, each one the size of a selenium " cell," the cell being an arrangement made with selenium, which varies in its electrical resistance according to the strength of the light illuminating it. This cell is held in one section of the bright image on the screen, then in the next, then in the next, and so on, until finally it has been held in the whole thousand sections. But each section is of a different brightness, according to what portion of the image is projected upon it. In each section, therefore, that the cell was held, its electrical resistance varied.

Now imagine you could record these variations in resistance on a similar screen at the receiving station. When the selenium cell was held over section 1 of the image of the screen, its resistance was, let us say, r_1; using a battery of 100 volts, and neglecting the resistance of any connecting lines, the current at the receiving station would be $\frac{100}{r_1}$. Let this regulate, in any imaginable way, the strength of an electric light, which is shining on a similar screen at the receiving station, on the screen being placed a sheet of sensitive photographic paper. Next let the selenium cell be held in the section 2, so that a slightly different part of the image falls upon it, the resistance changing to r_2, and the current at the receiving station to $\dfrac{100}{r_2}$; simultaneously let the electric lamp (whose brilliance has of course changed in the proportion of r_1 to r_2), shine on section 2 of the receiving screen. If you can imagine this procedure to be carried out over the whole photograph at the sending station, the ever-varying electric lamp being shone on always corresponding sections of the photographic paper at the receiving station, the movements being in all cases synchronous, you will be able to see that on developing the sheet of paper a photograph would be obtained, consisting of a thousand square patches of different intensity, which, examined from a distance, would give a representation of the original image projected on the screen. Such a process would in practice be both absurd and impossible, but it enables one to form some conception of the idea of Bidwell and Ayrton and Perry.

The image to be telegraphed could quite easily be a photograph printed on a transparent material, such as celluloid, and this print fixed to a revolving glass cylinder, inside which was fixed an electric lamp, whose rays were concentrated so as to pass through one spot on the cylinder to a fixed selenium cell. On then revolving the cylinder and letting it also rise spirally, the pencil of light would traverse different consecutive parts of the picture, and the light falling on the selenium would, of course, vary in strict accordance. Such a method is practically similar to that actually used by Professor Korn, as will be seen on reading the next chapter.

Then, again, the current sent to the receiving station, which would depend at each instant on the density of the particular piece of photograph through which the pencil of light was passing, could be utilised to open or close a shutter through which another pencil of light could be admitted to a sensitive photographic film. Suppose this film on a cylinder revolving in a precisely similar fashion to the transmitting cylinder, and you have what practically amounts to Professor Korn's receiver.

The great practical difficulty arose, however, from the fact that selenium, unlike the feminine mind, could not change rapidly enough ; there are an immense number of different tones in one small strip of a photograph, and the constant changes in illumination were not at all well responded to by the selenium cell. The practical application of the method was destined to await Professor Korn's remarkably ingenious work on the compensation of the " lag " in selenium cells, which only became possible after much very ingenious mathematical and experimental work. Korn is a master mathe-

matician, and photo-telegraphy is one instance
where somewhat abstruse calculations on paper
turned out to be in perfect harmony with practical
work.

In referring to the methods of Amstutz, I will
quote from an interesting article by Mr. William
Gamble, that appeared twelve years ago in the first
number of *Penrose's Pictorial Annual*, of which he
is the editor. Briefly, he says, the process is this :
A photograph in relief (prepared in gelatine) is
fixed to something akin to a phonograph cylinder,
so that a stylus travels over its surface, rising and
falling as the picture passes beneath it. Instead
of producing sound, like the phonograph, it is made
to vary the strength of an electric current, which
passes over a telegraph wire and actuates a similar
stylus at the other end, which, bearing on a plate
bent round a revolving cylinder, cuts a reproduction of the original, but in a series of parallel lines
(the successive " turns " of the cylinders) which
gives the effect of a half-tone block. The stylus is
sharpened like a graving tool, V-shaped, so that
as it cuts deeper it cuts wider, and in printing
produces darker or wider lines.

Amstutz, in a lengthy letter which the editor of
the *Annual* publishes, describes a method in which
a photographic print is made on a metallic sheet,
the half-tone of the photograph being broken up
into parallel lines, " the photo-message being re-

ceived at the distant station in an *engraved* manner ready for printing."

"Theoretically," he says, "the half-tone system encounters no difficulties whatever. From a practical point it is not available for commercial work." He describes the troubles that would arise from interference effects, owing to the lack of correspondence that there would be between the mesh of the half-tone screen and the path travelled by the stylus over the cylinder, and claims that by using the single-line pictures referred to these troubles could be avoided.

In all the half-tone photo-telegraphic work single-line pictures are solely used, but at present no satisfactory method has been obtained of engraving the block direct during the reception.

Amstutz's idea of using a photographic image in relief, and making the actual relief mechanically vary an electrical resistance, has been successfully followed up by a French inventor named Belin, but he again cannot obtain direct engraving at the receiving end.

Direct photo-engraving by telegraphy may "come" some day, but not until that much desired thing has been discovered, the variable relay. The resistance of a telephone line two hundred miles long may be, perhaps, 2,000 ohms. We cannot employ very high voltages, 100 volts being considered very high; if we divide 100 by 2,000, we get the maximum amount of current that could be obtained at the receiving station—one-twentieth of an ampère; with ·05 ampère and only therefore 5 watts, it would be almost impossible to actuate a graving tool, even to cut into some soft composition. Block-making is so rapidly done in a modern illustrated newspaper office that such a method is not now worth following up.

Turning next to Caselli's *pan-telegraph*, we find him employing a sheet of metal with a sketch or writing drawn upon it in insulating ink ; the sketch on metal was stretched over a curved copper plate, and a similar curved plate was placed at the receiving station, a sheet of paper moistened with potassium ferricyanide solution being stretched over it. The plates were electrically rocked, synchronism being obtained by means of a pendulum. A metal stylus traced over the sketch at one end and over the paper at the other, the circuit being completed through the metal plates. At the end of each " rock " the paper and sketch were shifted laterally, so that in each case the stylus travelled over a line parallel to the last line traced. When the sending style touched the metal the current flowed and the ferricyanide was decomposed, a blue mark being produced. Some excellent transmissions of writing, etc., were obtained in this way at a comparatively high rate of speed. The same system was employed by the French telegraph engineer, Meyer, except that he used synchronously revolving cylinders in place of the curved metal plates.

Although the transmission of writing cannot be classed with the telegraphy of photographs, it will be, nevertheless, of interest to describe the telewriter, which gives a facsimile reproduction at the receiving station of anything written or sketched at the sending station. In writing any letter on paper, the movement of the pen can always be resolved into horizontal and vertical components ; by making these resolved movements mechanically vary two resistances, currents of two corresponding strengths can be transmitted to a receiving instrument ; but three lines are necessary, or two lines and an earth.   The two currents when received are used to actuate a V-shaped nib filled with ink, both vertically and horizontally, the resultant movement causing the nib to trace over the paper a replica of whatever the transmitter draws with his mechanical " pen." In the telautograph of Grzanna, the two currents corresponding to the vertical and horizontal movements of the transmitting pen are made to actuate a mirror galvanometer, the mirror of which can turn about two axes, so that a spot of light traces the letters or sketch over a sheet of photographic paper.

These methods are only suitable for transmitting sketches, or designs that are drawn at the actual time of transmission. A cartoon was in one instance drawn by Mr. W. K. Haselden in Manchester and sent by him to the London office of the *Daily Mirror*, but it was not so satisfactory as the same sketch would have been had it been photographed and then telegraphed to London ; the pencil of the transmitter requires some practice to use it with comfort.

A method more recently worked out for the transmission of photographs is that of Charbonelle, a French postal engineer, in which once again the Caselli transmitter is employed, and a series of short currents are transmitted which correspond to the interruptions caused by the insulating lines of a sketch or single-line screen half-tone photograph. He has also endeavoured to transmit by a method that has been put to the test by almost every engineer who has paid any attention to the problem of photo-telegraphy, namely, by causing the deposit of silver (or other substance) in the image of a photographic film to act as the means of varying the current transmitted. This was very carefully investigated by the author in 1907, about a year before the publication of Charbonelle's patent, but although results of a kind were obtained, the idea was abandoned owing to certain fundamental difficulties which will probably never be overcome.

In Fig. 2 is seen a diagrammatic representation of a transverse section of the film of an ordinary

photographic negative. Let S be a stylus travelling over the film ; now consider any points
PQR, it being supposed that the film has been
coated on metal foil instead of glass or celluloid.
If one terminal of a battery be connected to S, the
other to the metal foil, current will flow from S to
P, in one instance the reduced silver grains forming the image being represented by dots.   Now
suppose the stylus to be at S', where, owing to a
light part of the picture, there is much less deposit
of silver.   Assuming the film to be of gelatine (in
a moist condition),
less current will
flow from S' to R
than from S to
P, as between S
and P there are

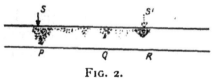

FIG. 2.

many more granules of silver to render the film
more conductive. Hence, if the photograph be
rotated on a cylinder, and the stylus trace a spiral
path over its surface, the current flowing through it
to a receiver should vary in accordance with the
depth of silver deposit.   I also tried using a relief
carbon image on copper foil, the gelatine being
saturated with a badly conducting medium, so that
the current passing from style to copper base would
vary inversely as the thickness of the film ; some
fair results were obtained in this way, but the
method, would be always very uncertain, as the

current would pass through the film in the line of least resistance.

Charbonelle's receiver is also one that has been suggested by some of the earlier workers ; he passes the received current into a microphone, in the centre of the diaphragm of which is a hardened point ; this point of course vibrates in the same manner as the diaphragm. The microphone is brought down over the cylinder of the receiving apparatus until it presses on an outer sheet of paper wrapped round it ; under this outer paper is, first, a sheet of carbon paper, and second, another sheet of plain paper. As the microphone diaphragm vibrates in response to the interruptions of the current, so the point digs into the outer paper and the mechanical pressure causes a carbon mark on the inner paper. The results are stated to be good, but the method is not likely to be of use for long distances.

Berjonneau has worked out a method of transmitting half-tone photographs made with a single-line screen, the receiver containing a minute shutter which cuts off or allows to pass the rays from a lamp concentrated on a revolving sensitive film. I have seen a promising result obtained with his apparatus,* but detailed particulars of his system are not yet available. He has, however, made transmissions over a telegraph line from Paris to Eng-

* Shown at Soc. Ing. Civ., Paris.

hien ".in four minutes seven seconds," according
to a newspaper report, "and the reproduction at
Enghien did not show any signs of lines, and might
have been made in the studio of a photographer."

An ingenious idea for transmission without wires
deserves mention here, and has been patented by
the inventor, Francesco de' Bernochi, of Turin. The
invention can never be of much practical value, and
is, in fact, a retrograde one, carrying us back to the
early experiments in wireless telephony by means

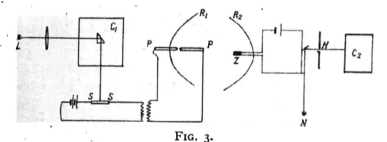

FIG. 3.

of light waves. The apparatus can be followed by
glancing at Fig. 3. Here C_1 is a glass cylinder
with a transparent photographic film wrapped round
it, and light from the lamp L, after passing through
a small portion of it, is reflected by a prism on to
a selenium cell SS. This is in series with a battery
and the primary of a form of induction coil. As
light of different intensities falls on the selenium
cell, whose resistance alters in proportion, current
is induced in the secondary of the coil and influ-
ences an arc lamp, on whose circuit it is shunted ;

this arc, the poles of which are represented in the diagram by PP, is placed at the focus of a parabolic reflector R_1, and its rays are therefore reflected as a parallel beam to the receiving reflector R_2. At the focus of this second reflector is a selenium cell Z, whose resistance is altered by the light falling upon it from the reflector. This cell is in series with a battery and mirror galvanometer, light from a lamp N being reflected by the mirror on to a graduated aperture H; the collected light is focussed upon a photographic film attached to the drum C_2, which revolves synchronously with the transmitting cylinder C_1.

The idea is an ingenious one, and might be made to work in practice over distances of a few hundred yards, but not more. A suggestion was made on somewhat similar lines to these to the author by Mr. Sharman, in reference to Korn's selenium machines, but for the purposes of wireless telegraphy the fluctuations in the resistance of the selenium would be used to influence the undamped oscillations given out by a singing arc, and a suitable receiver would record these fluctuations photographically.

One other possible means of receiving from any form of transmitter over short distances deserves reference, inasmuch as it has recently received the attention of Rignoux and Fournier for their proposed television apparatus. It is well known that if μ be the refractive index of a substance, and ϕ the angle of polarisation for that substance, the relation holds good.

$$\mu = \tan \phi.$$

If a liquid substance contained in a tube BC (Fig. 4) be subjected to a field produced by a coil through which current is passing, its refractive index will be changed; hence ϕ will be changed also. If rays of monochromatic light from a lamp L pass through one nichol prism N_1, then

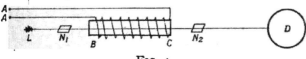

FIG. 4.

through the tube BC of liquid (carbon disulphide), afterwards passing through the analysing prism N_2 and thence to a photographic film attached to a receiving drum D, the nichols being set at the polarising angle, no light would reach the film *unless* a current passed through the coil round BC. The terminals of such a coil would be connected to the line AA, either directly or through a relay, and hence the film on D would record the impulses sent through the coil. The sensitiveness of such an apparatus would be very small unless a relay were employed, and this would at once put a limit on the speed of working, which would seriously hamper its utility.

P.T.   C

The commercial utility of photo-telegraphy only commenced after the adoption of Professor Korn's instruments by the *Daily Mirror*. Although his selenium machines were installed in Berlin and Paris at the same time, the *Daily Mirror* in London may be said to be the only journal that has utilised them, or any subsequent machine, in a really commercial way. Two of Korn's selenium machines were installed in Stockholm and Copenhagen in 1908, and some transmissions have been made by the newspapers which took up his system, but ever since their installation of the selenium instrument in November, 1907, the *Daily Mirror* has systematically carried out transmissions and has persistently endeavoured to develop the really practical side. The large amount of experimental work that I have carried out has been done entirely for the *Daily Mirror*, and the present state of efficiency of this new science is very largely due to the substantial help they have given to it.

This chapter has been written from a more or less historical standpoint, and it may therefore be said that the commercial or practical history commenced in 1907 with the use of Korn's selenium machines. The progress that has been made during the last two and a half years has been very considerable, and has been almost entirely due to paying the closest attention to small details. The mechanical parts of the various instruments have been made with greater precision, the physical theory of the selenium cell has been exhaustively worked out by Korn, who has also made a great deal of progress in determining the best form of string for the galvanometers used in photographic receivers. M. Chatenet, of *L'Illustration*, Paris, has done much valuable work in connection with the preparation of the line photographs for transmission, the importance of which will be seen later.

History does not dip into the future, fortunately for the historian, but it is quite clear by now that the telegraphy of photographs has a commercial value, and that this value will rapidly increase with the demands for pictures made on modern journalism. What other uses it will be put to remain to be seen, but there are many possibilities. As regards distance, where the cable renders transmission too slow, "wireless" may solve the problem, but that also remains to be seen.

Before closing this chapter, I should like to refer once more to Mr. Gamble's article in *Penrose's Pictorial Annual*, which it is interesting to recall to-day, since his predictions have been so well fulfilled.

"But suppose," he says, speaking of illustrated journalism, " it were possible to transmit the picture over the wires with the same facility as we now transmit the words, and suppose that the same

electric current rendered a transcript of the picture
in a form suited for immediately using or convert-
ing into a printing surface, what a revolution it
would effect in the methods of giving news to the
public, . . . of whose craving for illustrations
editors and publishers are fully conscious. 'Quite
so,' says the practical editor, 'but will such a thing
ever be possible? I doubt it.'

" Well, just to call to mind what electricity has
already given us besides telegraphy. By means of
this wonderfully potent power we transmit sound,
light, heat, and motive energy. Its latest and
perhaps most marvellous development is the utilisa-
tion of the so-called ' X-rays ' to enable us to probe
the mysteries of our anatomy and search for things
hidden from mortal eye. Surely it is but a little
step to annihilate the limitations of human vision
and provide us with a means of seeing things from
afar. *Undoubtedly this will be the next wonder
that electricity has in store for us.*"

Then, after describing Bain's chemical telegraph, in which at the transmitting station a metal
brush passed over large metal type letters and
closed a circuit which chemically reproduced the
letters at the receiving end, he says :

" I mention the foregoing chemical process,
because I think it will suggest to photographic
experimentalists a likely method of transmitting
pictorial records. For the letters of Bain's instru-

ment substitute a half-tone enamel print on copper showing alternate bare and covered parts, and the point then is to find a sufficiently sensitive transmitter."

The receiver is the part that remained to be made sufficiently sensitive, and I cannot help thinking the word " transmitter " was used for " receiver " by a slip. How this sensitiveness has been obtained will be explained in the chapter dealing with the telectrograph.

CHAPTER II.

PROFESSOR KORN'S SELENIUM PROCESS—EARLY
WORK WITH HIS ORIGINAL RECEIVER—THE
STRING GALVANOMETER — SYNCHRONISM —
FIRST EXPERIMENTS—THE EARLY HISTORY
OF COMMERCIAL PHOTO-TELEGRAPHY.

THE metal selenium is, in its crystalline state,
very sensitive to light. It has been utilised in
many instances of light telephony, from which it is

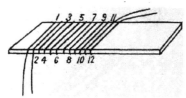

FIG. 5.

obvious that it is sen-
sible of extremely rapid
changes in the illumi-
nation.

The selenium *cell*,
so-called, takes the
form shown in Fig. 5; on a thin rectangular slab of
slate, steatite, or some other suitable material, two
coils of platinum wire are wound, one coil being
wound " inside " the other, so that no turn touches
another turn; thus, in the figure, turns 1, 3, 5, 7,
9 . . . belong to one coil, while turns 2, 4, 6, 8,
10 . . . belong to the other. We now fill in the
spaces between the turns with selenium, so that if
the resistance between turns 1 and 2 were R, and
there were n turns in each of the coils, the total

resistance of the " cell " would be approximately $\frac{R}{2n}$, assuming the number of turns very great and their distance apart equal. The dimensions of the

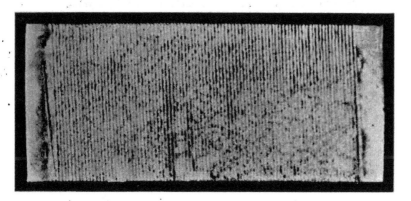

FIG. 6.

cells made by Giltay, of Delft, Holland, are about ·6·3 × 2·8 cm., and their resistance varies between very wide limits ; thus one may have a cell whose resistance is only 20,000 ohms, or one of $R = 250,000\ \Omega$. It seems to be a general rule that the greater the resistance of the cell the smaller its inertia, but it is by no means always the case.

The selenium has to be kept at a definite high temperature until it assumes the crystalline, slate-coloured form, when it becomes electrically conductive and sensitive to light. The light is apparently absorbed and made to do work in lessening the resistance ; the physical change is not relaxed—

the original state not restored—immediately the action of the light is discontinued ; the return to normal condition is thus not instantaneous; there is a *lag,* whilst over-illumination and excessive illumination may cause some long-sustained effect which has been conveniently termed fatigue. In Fig. 6 is seen an actual photograph of a selenium cell.

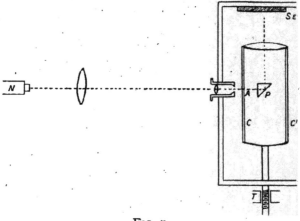

FIG. 7.

The difficulties caused by these characteristics of the selenium cells will be readily understood when we see how the cells are employed by Korn in his system.. I shall therefore describe the sending instrument in its simplest form, after which we can come back again to physical considerations.

The principal portion of the sending apparatus is shown in Fig. 7. Here the light from a Nernst lamp N is concentrated by the necessary lens system on to the glass cylinder CC', so that the rays cross at the point A where the pencil meets the first surface of the cylinder. A transparent photograph printed on a celluloid or gelatine film is wrapped round the cylinder, so that at A the light passes through one small point of it; it travels thence into the 45° prism P, by which it is reflected upwards upon a selenium cell SE. The glass cylinder is attached to a shaft with a screw thread, which turns in a fixed threaded collar T, so that when revolved by a motor it rises and turns spirally. It is thus seen that the spot of light at A in effect traces a spiral path over practically the whole photograph in due course. The intensity of the light at any instant depends on the density of the photographic film in the portion traversed at that instant, so that the light falling upon the selenium cell is always varying in accordance with the density of the photograph.

The " point " embraced by the light pencil at A is in reality about 3 × 2 mm. in area, hence no small details can be transmitted as several would be embraced at once by the beam. This is the reason why only portraits or very simple subjects could be transmitted by the selenium machines.*

---

* More complicated pictures have been transmitted by Korn's selenium machine by enlarging up the subject and dividing it into three or four parts, telegraphing each separately and then joining up the telegraphed components.

The size of the glass cylinders used is 13 cm. length by 7 cm. diameter, so the picture transmitted is 22 × 13 cm. The pitch of the thread on the axle is 1 mm., so that the cylinder turns 130 times during a complete transmission ; it revolves once in 5 seconds, hence the time of transmission is just over 11 minutes. Arrangements were provided in some of the machines to double the pitch of the axle thread, so that a photograph could be telegraphed in under 6 minutes. This, of course, meant a corresponding sacrifice of detail.

We must now return to the selenium cell and see how its slowness to respond to the variations in illumination cast upon it from the prism have been largely overcome by the ingenious system of " compensation " worked out and patented by Professor Korn prior to 1907. If a certain amount of light be falling upon the cell, so that its inertia be overcome, and its resistance be r_1, then any increment, δI in the illumination will give a decrement in the resistance, in a way connecting the reciprocals of the resistances r_1 and r_2 as follows :—

$$\frac{1}{r_2} = \frac{1}{r_1} + a\delta I,$$

or if the increase in illumination be used for only a short time t,

$$\frac{1}{r_2} = \frac{1}{r_1} + a\delta I f(t),$$

and $f(t)$ converges to 1 where $t = \infty$. $F(t)$ is a.

function of the time, and a is (in both cases) a constant depending on the selenium cell and its characteristics; a can, in fact, be termed the " sensitiveness " of the cell.

Professor Korn has shown that where β and m are inertia constants of the selenium cell the change in resistance y can be obtained for an increase in illumination δI from an equation of the form

$$\text{current} = y = a\delta I . \varepsilon - \beta t^{-\frac{1}{m}}$$

where $0 < m < \infty$; β is the inertia constant and

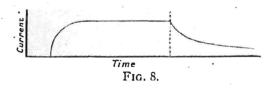

FIG. 8.

m the exponential inertia; for photo-telegraphic work m should be as small as possible, and this is obtained best by using platinum wire in the preparation of the cell and very pure selenium; m can be made as low as $\frac{2}{3}$.

The relation between time and current, shown as an inertia curve, is seen in Fig. 8. In the figure we see the effect of suddenly illuminating the cell for a time which, expressed as the abscissa, goes as far as the vertical dotted line; after the time t the illumination is cut off, but the resistance, instead of increasing again to normal instantly, takes a considerable time as indicated;

there is considerable lag, and it may actually take some seconds before the resistance becomes the normal for no illumination.

Now let us see what this means in actual photo-telegraphy. It has been seen that the transparent photograph revolves in cylindrical form, so that different consecutive parts of it intercept the light beam which, after reflexion in the prism, falls on the cell. Suppose a bright part in the photograph

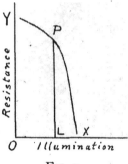

FIG. 9.

is adjacent to a very dark part, the light falling on the cell is great at the moment the bright part intercepts the light, and is very small immediately afterwards when the dark part takes its place. The current passed through the cell should increase with the bright part and instantly fall again when the dark part comes; instead, the lag in the cell intervenes, and it only half falls, and thus interferes fundamentally in the process.

Various means have been tried to counteract the

inertia, and to my mind the most successful is the method Korn has suggested of keeping the cell always sufficiently illuminated to overcome it. Thus suppose we represent the effect of light on resistance by a curve of the form shown in Fig. 9, the point P gives us the place on the curve after

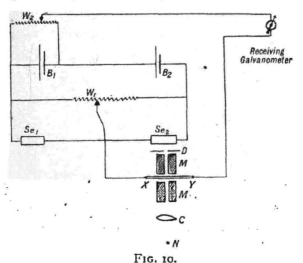

FIG. 10.

which for every increment of light δL the decrease in resistance in a small time t is $a\delta R$. If sufficient light OL be allowed always to fall on the cell so that the inertia YP is overcome, the effect of any additional light will be very rapid. The compensation method of Korn gives further a much brisker action, and the scheme is seen in Fig. 10.

Here the light which has traversed the revolving photograph falls on the selenium cell Se_1. This cell is placed as one arm of a Wheatstone bridge, a second cell Se_2 being placed on the opposite arm. W is a regulating resistance, and B_1 and B_2 two batteries of about 100 volts, B_1 being provided with a compensating variable resistance W_2. The galvanometer is of the "string" form, i.e., two fine wires XY move laterally in the field of a powerful electromagnet, whose pole pieces MM are tunnelled with a hole. A small piece of

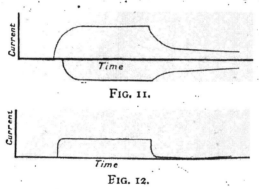

FIG. 11.

FIG. 12.

aluminium or magnesium foil is stuck to the wires in the centre, and this shutter just cuts off the light which would pass from a Nernst lamp N through the poles. If current passes through the wires they are laterally displaced, and the beam of light can then reach the second selenium cell Se_2. As the current transmitted to the receiving station passes there into a precisely similar galvanometer, the circuit is closed.

Now let us see what happens when a bright part

in the photograph causes light to be cast on the cell
Se_1. The equilibrium of the bridge is at once upset,
current therefore passes through XY, the shutter
is displaced, and light falls, a fraction of a second
later, on to Se_2. We can represent the effect for an
illumination I by the two curves below (Fig. 11)
on opposite sides of the time axis. Add the two
ordinates and you get the " dead beat " curve shown
in Fig. 12. The effect is almost instantaneous, and
when the illumination ceases the current drops at
once to zero. This effect can only be obtained,

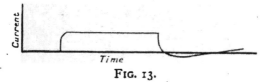

FIG. 13.

needless to say, when the two cells are well
matched ; it is easy to have over-compensation, as
shown in Fig. 13, where the current is brought
below zero, and time is thus lost in regaining a
normal condition.

It is not difficult to show that for good compensation, assuming the equations of the two cells be

$$\text{(i) } y_1 = a_1 \Delta I . e^{-\beta_1 t^{-\frac{1}{m}}}$$

$$\text{(ii) } y_2 = a_2 \Delta I . e^{-\beta_2 t^{-\frac{1}{m_2}}}$$

we must have the condition fulfilled

$$\frac{d \cdot (y_1 - y_2)}{dt} = 0,$$

and that for this we must have

$$a_1 \beta_1 = a_2 \beta_2.$$

Both cells should have m as nearly equal as possible and very small—the principal cell Se_1 should have great sensitiveness and small inertia; the compensating cell Se_2 should have proportionately small sensitiveness and large inertia, so that we can fulfil approximately the condition

$$a_1 \beta_1 = a_2 \beta_2.$$

A rather interesting point is raised by the fact that, according to Rühmer, it is possible to sensitise a selenium cell for a narrow region of the spectrum. He had utilised cells of different colour sensitiveness with a view to duplex wireless telephony, but it occurred to the author that possibly by colour sensitising a cell and using light only of the colour for the particular illumination the inertia might be less, and possibly the sensitiveness higher; with a cell of " dark resistance " r, the maximum useful amount of illumination only lowers this to perhaps $\frac{r}{2}$ or $\frac{r}{3}$, though one can obtain cells with a very large a, so that the ratio $\dfrac{\text{resistance when dark}}{\text{resistance when illumined}}$ is as much as 4 : 1 or 5 : 1. Thus a cell of resistance 250,000 ohms will sometimes become reduced in resistance to about 60,000 when illuminated with a 16 candle-power lamp held 3 inches away from it. The

maximum sensitiveness is towards the yellow-
orange portion of the spectrum, but the inertia
appears to be unaffected by the wave-length,
though Korn has patented the method of using a
selected colour. Several experiments were made
in England screening the light with colour filters,
so that light of known wave-lengths
was used for illuminating the cells.
The results of a series of measure-
ments showed that there was no
advantage, the lag being the same
as when ordinary Nernst light was
employed..

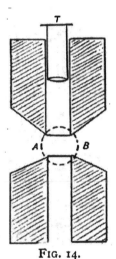

FIG. 14.

Before describing the actual receiving apparatus of Korn's selenium machines it will be of interest
to see the construction of the galvanometer, to which he has given
so much attention, and which is of
extreme sensitiveness, especially
when of the modified form as used in his later "telautograph" (see next chapter). The field magnets are
powerful, and the pole pieces measure about
5 × 11 × 4 cm. These converge nearly to points
in the centres, as shown in Fig. 14. Thus they
nearly touch at AB, only sufficient room being left
for two fine silver wires to move freely between
them. The hole through the poles is shown in the
diagram, and a sliding tube T fitted with a small

P.T.   D

short focus lens is provided in the hole nearest the receiving box. The shadow of a magnesium shutter (described later) attached to the wires can be sharply focussed upon a diaphragm by sliding the tube T to the correct position.

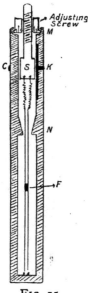

FIG. 15.

A metal collar (indicated by the dotted circle) is fixed above the pole-pieces into which the moving part of the galvanometer is fitted; this part is shown separately in Fig. 15. The outside portion of this (MN) is a cylindrical tube which fits into the collar. A sliding piece S is free to move up and down inside the tube, and is fitted with a screw thread, over which a graduated adjusting nut is placed. By turning this regulating screw, S is moved up or down and the tension on the wires varied. The wires, about $\frac{1}{1000}$th inch thick, are attached to two very fine springs (of the same material) fitted to S. The small shutter F, about 2 × 1·5 mm. in area, and as thin as possible, is gummed to the wires so that it comes on the optic axis when the piece is fitted into the magnet collar. The sliding portion S is insulated from the brass tube, but is connected with a contact K. This contact and another metal button C fit against two corresponding contacts in the field magnet collar, which are in turn connected with the sliding contacts of the resistances already described.

The weight of the " moving part " of the galvanometer is almost negligible, its moment of inertia extremely small, and with the length of wires used a period of swing as small as $\frac{1}{1200}$th of a second can be obtained.   The current flows in at C and traverses the fine wires upwards from bottom to top, leaving them at K.   The field due to each is thus similar, hence their displacement is lateral, and is approximately equal to

$$C \left(\frac{1}{r_1} - \frac{1}{r_2} \right) \times \text{constant of galvanometer.}$$

We may regard the wires as elastic substances stretched across the apparatus, where the displacement D can be represented by $f(e)$, or some function of the elasticity; the wires can be set in vibration, and if one impulse be given by passing a sudden short period current through the wires, when displaced thereby through a distance D they have sufficient potential energy to cause them to swing back past the position of rest through a distance slightly smaller than D in the same manner as a pendulum.   This is clearly shown by the photographic records (p. 110) obtained of the movements of the shutter F recorded under various circumstances on a moving photographic film. This period can be made shorter by using shorter "strings" or wires, but as there is a practical limit to their fineness, we must make the factor e increase by the strings becoming shorter ; hence the current necessary to displace them an equal amount becomes greater, and where selenium is used its resistance is so high that a limit is immediately set to the length of strings practicable. The magnetic field may of course be increased when the galvanometer constant K in the expression $D = CK \left(\dfrac{1}{r_1} - \dfrac{1}{r_2} \right)$ becomes greater. The Einthoven galvanometer, of which Korn's apparatus is a special form, is often provided with a far greater field than he employs.

Once in each revolution of the receiving drum there is a distinct kick in the galvanometer, as for the synchronising of the sending and receiving apparatus it is necessary, as will be seen later, to cut the current out of the galvanometer circuit and switch it into the synchronising gear. This kick, due to a capacity discharge from the line, was to some extent overcome by Korn by shunting a small resistance across the galvanometer at the terminals K, C. To facilitate its regulation I replaced this fixed resistance by a regulating shunt resistance of 0 to 50 ohms, but it was ultimately found that the kick could be best avoided by very careful adjustment of the position of the fleeting contact through which the synchronising current passed.

The shadow of the galvanometer foil is cast
upon a triangular aperture in a diaphragm E
(Fig. 16), being magnified up a good many
times by the lens T which is fitted into one pole
of the electro-magnet. This shadow prevents
the light from the lamp N reaching the small
lens O which concentrates a real image of the
aperture (when illuminated) upon the photographic film ; this revolves on the drum D, the

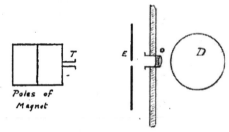

Poles of
Magnet

FIG. 16.

drum being fitted into a small light-tight wooden
box.   Now if the shutter is displaced, the shadow
moves to one side, and light immediately passes
through the aperture at E and exposes the film.
The more the shadow moves towards the base of
the triangular hole, the greater is the light which
reaches the film ; by using a triangular instead of a
square hole the effect of movement of the shutter
on the light transmitted to the film is obviously
amplified, and this amplification is necessary
because the ratio of illumination to resistance of

the selenium in the sending apparatus is not constant, but decreases as the illumination increases. The angle at the apex of the triangle has some-

FIG. 17.—Photograph of galvanometer as used by Prof. Korn.

times to be altered to suit a particular cell, but is usually about 50° to 60°. The shutter, and hence the shadow on E, is constantly moving more or less towards the base of the triangle according to the strength of the current and therefore to the density

of the photograph being transmitted. The area
of the picture received is one quarter that of the
film used in transmission.

The method of synchronising the sending and
receiving cylinders now requires explanation. A
small error in synchronisation will cause distortion
of the picture received, and great care is required

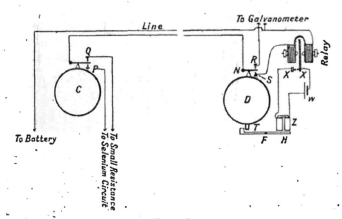

FIG. 18.

to ensure its accurate adjustment. In Fig. 18
let us suppose that C is the cylinder of the transmitting apparatus, and D the receiving drum.
There is a projecting pin on the bottom of the
transmitting cylinder which once in each revolution strikes against a contact spring, throwing
it away from contact with P and *into contact*
with Q. When the spring is in contact with
P—during practically the whole revolution—the

selenium circuit flows through the line to the receiver. When it is displaced and connects with Q, the current from the battery has merely to pass through a small fixed resistance, about one-tenth that of the selenium, so that the current is some ten times as great. As soon as the cylinder has turned a little more, the spring returns into contact with P again.

Now at the receiving machine we have a similar pin which throws over a spring N from contact with R into contact with S. Whereas R leads to the galvanometer, S leads to one coil of a relay as shown, the other coil of the relay being connected with the other unit of the line, together with the other end of the galvanometer.

What happens then is that every time the pin on the sending cylinder throws the spring against the contact Q, a strong current is transmitted through the line. If at that instant the corresponding spring N of the receiver be also thrown against S, the current received passes into the relay instead of into the string galvanometer.

By making the drum D turn quicker than the cylinder C it will obviously reach the end of its revolution first. It is then suddenly stopped by the check T, which strikes against a movable steel check F. When the slower turning sending cylinder has finished *its* revolution, the strong current is sent, as we have seen, into the relay, exciting the coils and causing the small magnetised armature to be attracted towards the left side in the diagram. The platinum contacts XX then touch, and current from the local battery passes through the magnet Z. This attracts the armature H, so that the check turns about the fulcrum F into a position such that T is free to move and the drum consequently again starts running.

The motive mechanism driving the drum cannot of course stop and start abruptly at the end of each revolution, a friction clutch is therefore provided, as shown

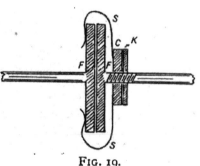

FIG. 19.

in the next diagram (Fig. 19). The shaft is cut through and two parallel faces FF fitted, springs SS being attached to the lower one which grip the upper one. When the motion of the cylinder is checked, the two faces turn one against the other. The springs are fixed to a collar C which can be screwed over the threaded shaft, K being a lock nut. The tension of the friction clutch can thus be regulated.

The transmitting cylinder is, as already stated, revolved at about the rate of one revolution in five seconds, or in reality at about $\frac{99}{100}$ths of this speed ; as the receiving drum must revolve quicker, in order to be stopped and then restarted by the synchronism signal of the transmitter after each complete revolution, it is run at about $\frac{101}{100}$ths of the speed. There is thus a difference of 2 per cent. in the rates of the two, which means an unavoidable elongation of the received image.

The regulation of the motors is carried out by means of regulating resistances and frequency metres. The motor acts to a small extent as a dynamo, as two sections of the armature are connected to slip rings with brushes fitted, so that an alternating current is derived from them. This alternating current is supplied to an electro-magnet, whose polarity at one pole-piece therefore changes twice in each revolution of the armature. A row of tuned steel magnetised springs is fixed in front of the pole-piece, fixed at the base and free to vibrate vertically. These springs are thus attracted and repulsed at each revolution of the motor, and if a certain spring among them be cut to such a length that its period is equal to the period of the alternating current, it will vibrate very freely, while other springs not in tune will not vibrate at all.

Now several such springs, so cut that their periods range from 97 per second to 103 per second, are fixed at their lower ends in front of the pole-piece of the electro-magnet. By means of the regulating switch of the motor — an ordinary variable resistance in series with the field magnets —the motor can be speeded up until, say, the spring labelled 99 vibrates freely. The motor is then revolving $\frac{99}{2}$ times a second, or just under 3,000

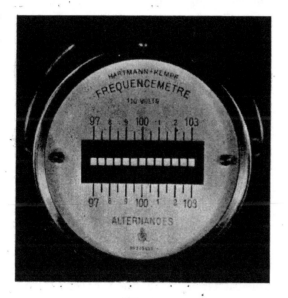

FIG. 20.

times per minute. This is the condition for the motor of the sending apparatus. The face of the meter is shown in Fig. 20.

Similarly at the receiving station the operator runs his motor at just over 3,000 revolutions per minute. Each motor is geared down with a worm drive in oil, which has to work very sweetly in order to prevent vibration. In many later models of photo - telegraphic apparatus the motors are mounted on separate stands and connected to the driving gear by flexible shafting.

The relay used by Professor Korn for utilising the synchronising current to close the magnetic

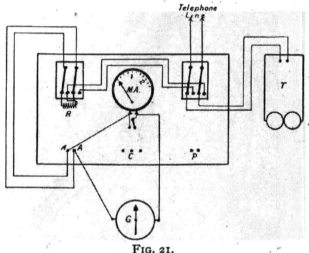

FIG. 21.

check release circuit is a Siemens & Halske polar-ised relay. A polarised relay is not necessary unless it be sufficiently sensitive to work with a current equal in intensity to the line current for the galvanometer. The Siemens & Halske relay can be rendered more or less sensitive at will by regulating the distance of one magnet from the armature it has to attract, keeping the other magnet fixed.

The whole arrangement of Professor Korn's selenium instruments has now been described, and there remains only the description of the actual commercial working to be given. It is clear that there must be some means of communication between the operators of the sending and receiving machines. As a metallic circuit is necessary owing to the weakness of the current transmitted, telephone lines are, employed, and these must be quite isolated and free from annunciators or shunts. A convenient arrangement is made by which the operator can switch at will the line into his instrument or into the telephone. The switchboard is shown in Fig. 21.

There are two change-over telephone switches on the board as shown. The change-over contacts of one are connected to two terminals AA, which lead to the receiving machine, denoted by G for convenience. One of these lines passes first through the milliampère metre MA to indicate the strength of the line current. The change-over contacts of the other switch go to the telephone line. It will be seen that when the switches are in the position shown the telephone line goes direct to the telephone T, and the machine terminals are in connection with a 1,000 Ω resistance R. When switched over towards the right the machine is in connection with the telephone line, and the telephone instrument is out of circuit. The three terminals C give

100 and 200 volts to the selenium cells in the manner already shown in the compensation diagram, while current is led from P to the motor and galvanometer magnets.

It is hardly necessary to say that accumulators

FIG. 22.—Prof. Korn at the telephone, when awaiting the first picture from Paris in 1907.

are essential in order to ensure smooth running and constant current.

Much trouble is experienced with some selenium cells, while others will last without any bother for many months. The " fatigue " often spoken of is really a permanent lag in the cells; a definite physical change appears gradually to take place in the selenium with the result that they are less sensitive to light, and the ratio of their "light sensitiveness" to "dark sensitiveness" becomes less. They are sometimes enclosed in glass cells which are sealed and exhausted, but this is not done in the case of Professor Korn's machines. A cell is liable sometimes to get into a certain state which renders the current "intermittent," *i.e.,* continuous but always variable, the variation amounting perhaps to 10 or 20 per cent. This trouble would appear to be due to bad contact somewhere, but it is in reality a fault of certain old cells. The most successful working of the selenium machines was obtained after

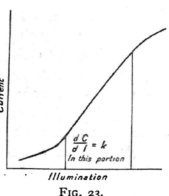

FIG. 23.

adopting the method patented in 1908 by Professor Korn for keeping the cell always slightly illuminated, so that the inertia was overcome. If the curve given in Fig. 23 represent the effect of light of increasing intensity upon the current (or reciprocal resistance of the cell), then that portion of the curve shown would be the best to use for photo-telegraphy, where the ratio $\frac{C}{I}$ is more or less constant; that part of the curve to the left of the first vertical line represents the amount of light continually falling on the cell before any additional illumination from the photographic transparency falls upon it. Within the portion selected $\frac{\delta C}{\delta I}$ is almost constant, and on it will depend largely the shape of the triangular aperture in the receiving diaphragm.

The first photograph wired by Korn's new selenium machines was received from Berlin at the office of the French illustrated weekly paper, *L'Illustration*, in October, 1907. . It was a photograph of President Fallières, and came through with considerable success. The first night of the trials Berlin-Paris, Professor Korn and his wife, his assistant. Herr Will, and several post office officials, and some of the leading newspaper men of Paris, were present. As the telephone lines were to be required for an hour or two, it was necessary to make the experiments very late, and the line was promised for midnight. After some minutes we got the connection with Berlin, but there was an annunciator bridged across it, and we could get practically no current at Paris. Every effort was made by the Director of Telephones, and we all waited patiently until after two o'clock in the morning, with no result, and finally everyone was obliged to leave, feeling both tired and disappointed.

On the next occasion, however, the picture of

Fallières was received, and a photograph wired to Berlin from Paris. At Berlin Dr. Glatzel was in charge, the instrument being installed at the office of the *Lokal Anzeiger*.

A few days later Professor Korn left for London, leaving M. Chatenet at Paris as operator, and I brought the *Daily Mirror* instrument with me to London. The Paris and London instruments had been made by J. Carpentier, the well-known scientific instrument maker of the Maison Rhumkorff.

FIG. 24.—One of the first photographs wired by Korn's compensated selenium machines.

The Paris-London photo-telegraphic service was inaugurated on November 7th, 1907, when Professor Korn received the first photograph from Paris at the *Daily Mirror* office. Every facility was then and has since been given by the officials of the General Post Office, and much courtesy has been shown throughout by Major O'Meara, Mr. F. Tandy, and other of the chief telephone engineers of this country. The two above officials were

P.T. E

present at the first Paris-London trial, and attended the lecture given by Professor Korn on that

FIG. 25

occasion. The photograph first wired to London was one of King Edward VII., and it is reproduced in Fig. 25. The original was an exceed-

ingly good photograph, eminently suited to
the selenium process, and it is a peculiar
fact that, as far as an actual face is concerned, that photograph still remains the most
perfect ever transmitted, putting aside the purely
technical peculiarity of the stripes or bands of which
it is composed.   These lines in the photograph
correspond to the threads of the screw axle on which
depends the upward travel of the receiving drums,
and they make an angle with a line drawn horizontally across the greatest length of the picture of
approximately $\sin^{-1}\left(\dfrac{1}{465}\right)$. The lines can be got
rid of by placing the small lens which concentrates
the light from the triangular diaphragm upon the
film at a greater distance from the film, but the
sharpness of definition of the photograph then at
once suffers.   This may sometimes be all the better
in the case of a portrait where the diffusion renders
the result much more " photographic."   But the
sharpest definition is necessary where any attempt is
made to telegraph a picture with any small detail
in it.   " Small detail " is in itself a limited term,
as only very bold and simple subjects can be transmitted with apparatus of this size, and hence its
almost exclusive application to the telegraphy of
portraits.   The lens above referred to should cast
an image of the triangular aperture on the film
which is almost a point.

More contrast could be got in the received pictures by placing over the diaphragm a graduated glass, made by exposing a photographic plate to a fixed light some distance away and gradually uncovering it, so that on development one end is very dense, the other very transparent, density graduating into transparency. By cementing such a glass to the diaphragm so that at the apex you have a dense part gradually becoming more transparent as you approach the base, the effect is to get far more light through as the shutter uncovers the triangular hole than would be the case otherwise.

About the time of the first trials with Korn's selenium apparatus, the submarine telephone lines linking this country with France were rather faulty, and it was only occasionally that we were able to have line for experimental purposes. The average business telephone call lasts six minutes, and in these early days we wanted it for at least half an hour; hence, when one or more lines were " down," the pressure on the others was so great that the telephone authorities were quite unable to give us the use of one. The consequence was that experiments were few and far between, and often we found the line—quite good for the purposes of ordinary telephony—unsuitable for our own trials. This state of affairs continued for some months, but in the spring matters improved, and we were able to make numerous experiments, generally obtaining

Fig. 26.

the line for about half-an-hour soon after eight o'clock. The results were affected by various factors, the chief of them being leakance. Three-quarters of a milliampère is about the minimum current possible to work with, and we frequently only received about half. The optical arrangements could, of course, be easily modified to compensate for this, but unless the tension in the galvanometer strings was above a certain figure, its action was uncertain.

Induction from other lines was very marked at certain times, and at first it was thought that this was due to weather conditions. The observed facts, however, showed this not to be the case ; induction effects were chiefly due to line conditions. The two systems of telegraphy, Morse and Baudot, gave marked induction effects, and telegraphic experts declared they could actually read Morse messages on some of the photographs. Induction effects can be seen on looking at the photograph shown in Fig. 26, where they cross the photograph at regular intervals.

The photographic image, as will have been gathered, consists really of one long spiral line of varying thickness and intensity, which becomes resolved into parallel lines when the image is changed from its cylindrical form and laid out flat. The thickness of the line is increased by the induction, hence the dots and dashes are graphically represented in the received photograph.

In the Baudot telegraphic system there is a periodic current, and the stripes seen are at regular intervals across the picture. These marks were at first presumed to be due to some mechanical trouble.

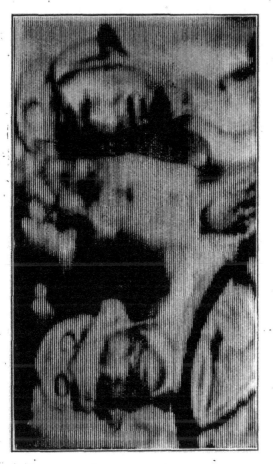

FIG. 27.—Example of a news photograph sent from Paris.

Photographs telegraphed from Paris now became a fairly regular feature in the *Daily Mirror*, and a

great many people, among them some of our leading scientific men, began to watch the results with
curiosity.   Some of them doubtless wondered
whether the system would ever have much commercial utility, and the limit set to the process
owing to one being confined to the transmission of
portraits made this easily understood.   It was not
until the installation of Korn's telautograph (see
next chapter) that the enormous possibilities of
photo-telegraphy became clear.

The Franco-British Exhibition took place in
1908, opening in May, and the selenium machines
were exhibited there by the *Daily Mirror* in a small
pavilion erected for the purpose.   The drawback
to such a method of demonstration was that, beyond
watching the movement of the galvanometer shutter
and the revolving photographic transparency, little
was to be seen.   A trunk line was installed, and
photographs were received from Paris at the pavilion each evening that the line was available.   A
picture of the King was transmitted at four o'clock
on the afternoon when His Majesty formally opened
the exhibition.

The great fire which occurred in September,
1908, and burnt the Paris telephone exchange to
the ground, will doubtless be remembered.   This
effectually put a stop to photo-telegraphic experiments, and little more was done except to give
demonstrations to the visitors.   As a general rule

the whirring noise of the motors excited the curiosity of people outside the little pavilion, and large crowds endeavoured to come inside, a queue some fifty yards long occasionally awaiting their turns outside. The pavilion would get so full that those farthest away from the barrier could see nothing. On one such occasion two elderly ladies squeezed their way in, and after waiting patiently some ten minutes and seeing nothing but the backs of other people they came out again, and the following conversation ensued :—

FIRST LADY: " How very wonderful it is ! "

SECOND LADY: " Extraordinary ! Marvellous ! "

FIRST LADY: " Did you see anything ? "

SECOND LADY: " No, I could see nothing. Did you see anything ? "

FIRST LADY: " Nothing."

The demonstrations continued until the close of the exhibition, by which time they badly needed overhauling. This took some time, and when finished, it was decided to instal one of them at Manchester, in order to facilitate the transmission to London of north-country pictures.

The instrument was placed at the offices of the *Manchester Courier*, the installation being as follows:—

One 80 ampère hour 110 volt set of accumulators, with charging board, etc., for the motor, lamp and magnet.

One 2 ampère hour 210 volt set of accumulators for the selenium cell line circuit.

Trunk Telephone and change-over switches as described.

The line from Manchester was shorter and more satisfactory for the selenium machine than the Paris-London line, and the results obtained were very fair. Photographs were frequently telegraphed to Manchester and published in the *Manchester Courier*, while every evening some portrait of topical interest was sent from Manchester to London. Soon after this service began, the Paris lines were again available, and the Paris-London service was again continued.

Several experiments were made with a view to transmitting landscapes or sporting pictures instead of simple portraits by dividing the original picture into two or three parts and telegraphing one part at a time, afterwards joining up the sections. This method is quite plausible in theory, but unfortunately only worked out in practice in the laboratory. Each portion takes twelve minutes to transmit, and often during such time the condition of the lines would vary sufficiently to render the next portion quite different in character. These differences could have been made good by *retouching*, had the time available permitted of it. But it must be remembered that where a photograph is telegraphed, it is usually sent at a late hour, and if much time be spent on the retouching, it may be too late for publication.

The public is very suspicious, and scientific men

are apt to ignore or disbelieve things with which they are not personally intimate, and the opinion, I know, prevailed at one time that many of the telegraphed pictures were greatly retouched or " faked " before they were printed in the paper. Let me say here, therefore, once for all, that telegraphed pictures have, of necessity, *less retouching than the ordinary photographs*, and unless they arrive over the wire tolerably good in quality they are absolutely useless. The idea that the results were faked arose from mere ignorance of the vital conditions under which commercial photo-telegraphy is possible.

The selenium machines were kept running at Manchester and Paris until Professor Korn had completed tests between Berlin and Paris with his telautograph. They served a useful purpose, as they inaugurated a new branch of electrical science which is destined to play an important part in modern illustrated journalism. An instance of the criminalistic possibilities of photo-telegraphy was shown in 1908, when a man named Hedemann, whose photograph was telegraphed from Paris to London and published in the *Daily Mirror*, was recognised by someone in London who knew him and gave important information to the police.

Professor Korn is at present endeavouring to render more satisfactory his compensation of the lag in the selenium cell, and eventually to prepare instruments based on selenium for experiments across the Atlantic. Herr Rühmer, whose work in connection with wireless telephony is well known, and who has contributed many valuable papers on the physical properties of selenium, claims now to have completely overcome inertia in certain new cells he has made. He is using selenium cells in experimental trials to transmit by electricity a visual image of an object or person, but as his work concerns television and not the telegraphy of pictures, it will not be discussed here.

CHAPTER III.

THE KORN TELAUTOGRAPH — PRINCIPLES OF WORKING—ADVANTAGES OVER SELENIUM— EARLY WORK WITH LINE PICTURES—EXPERIMENTS WITH TELEPHONE AND TELEGRAPH CABLES — RECENT PROGRESS WITH THE TELAUTOGRAPH.

THE telautograph as arranged by Professor Korn is really a combination of Caselli's transmitter with the Einthoven galvanometer and photographic receiver as used in the selenium machines. From the very first the stringent limitation to simple portraits dictated by the use of the selenium instruments was felt, and with the introduction of the telautograph a new and commercial field of work was opened up. There are doubtless a great number of important or interesting men and women in the world, but there are every day hundreds of interesting " news snapshots," and while portraits of the former become more or less exhausted at times, the " *photo d'actualité* " is always obtainable and commands interest.

The first function of the telautograph was to telegraph sketches or drawings in line, the sketches·

being drawn with a pen and some ink that was essentially an electric insulator upon a metal base. Thus the first materials sent to me by Professor Korn were some sheets of copper foil, a quill pen and some ink composed of an alcoholic solution of shellac strongly tinted with a violet aniline dye. Now, if we draw a sketch on copper with this ink, and connect the under side of it, *i.e.*, the plain

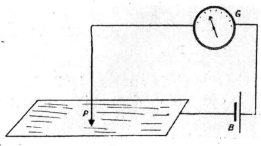

FIG. 28.

copper side, with one pole of an electric battery B (see Fig. 28), the other pole of which is connected to one terminal of a galvanometer G, and we connect the other galvanometer terminal with a pen P, this consisting of, say, a darning needle, and we now draw the " pen " slowly over the surface of the sketch, we shall see that whenever the pen crosses a line of the drawing, *i.e.*, a shellac line, the galvanometer needle is at zero, while when the pen is in contact with the bare metal—corresponding to the paper of an ordinary sketch—the galvanometer needle is deflected.

In this simple experiment you see the whole prin-
ciple of the telautograph, essentially different from
the system described in Chapter II. ; the galvanometer G represents the receiving apparatus, the
sketch on copper and the needle tracing over it
represent the transmitter. We shall now see how
this system works out in practice. A diagram-

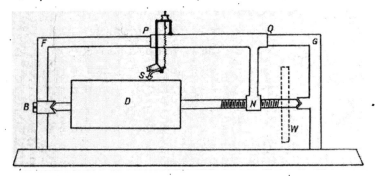

FIG. 29.

matic representation of the transmitter is shown in
Fig. 29.

On a substantial iron base two uprights are
fixed, and the metal drum D fits on flanges on
a steel shaft which turns between centres ; this
cylinder is turned true in the lathe. Along the
top is a cylindrical steel bar FG, and over this
slides a substantial tube PQ to which is fitted
the carrier of the steel " pen " or stylus. An
arm fitted with a half-nut N projects from one end
of the tube, and the right-hand part of the steel

shaft is cut with a thread, about 20 threads per centimetre ; W represents the cog wheel of the motive arrangement, so that as the shaft turns the nut N slides along and so imparts to the stylus S a lateral motion, hence the stylus traces a spiral path over the surface of the picture, which is fixed round the revolving drum D.

The motive power is again a motor with two slip rings fitted to the armature, so that alternating current is generated for the actuation of a frequency meter. The motor turns at 3,000 revolutions per minute, and the speed is geared down so that the cylinder revolves once in two seconds. As the receiving apparatus is placed on the same table as the transmitter, and contains as its essential part the string or Einthoven galvanometer, it was found necessary to mount the motor on a separate stand and to connect it with flexible shafting. In the most recent apparatus the motor and gear box are mounted together on a stand fixed rigidly to the wall, and flexible shafting connects the gear box with the cog wheel that engages with the wheel W shown in the diagram.

The dimensions of the cylinders used at London and Manchester are 63·5 mm. diameter and 130 mm. length. In the apparatus first installed by Professor Korn at Berlin and Paris he employed a small cylinder the same size as the receiving drum, but it is a considerable advantage to have the transmitting cylinder double the size of that used in the reception.

The stylus consists essentially of a finely-pointed needle, and ordinary gramophone needles set in a suitable holder have been used with success ; the best form of stylus is one originally designed by Mr. Sanger Shepherd, and its form is indicated in the diagram.   The stylus, made of steel or other suitable material, is of the shape shown, and has a small tube put through it about the middle, which acts as an axis.   Two needle-point bearings fit into this finely-drilled tube, so that it is free to turn with minimum friction; one end of the stylus is bent downwards and is pointed sharply, the other has a hole through it to which is attached a tension spring, so that the pressure of the style on the cylinder can be regulated. The sparking at the point of contact is apt, if not sufficiently well overcome, to quickly blunt the stylus, and Mr. Shepherd prepared several with iridium points let into the steel " head "; these proved very satisfactory, but were eventually replaced by a modification which was designed to facilitate the trial of needles of various materials, working at different angles to the surface of the drum.   This design is shown in Fig. 30.

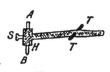

FIG. 30.

Here H is the head of the stylus, drilled so that a needle AB can be fitted into it and clamped by the screw S; TT is the finely-drilled tube into the ends of which the needle points fit. Steel needles, sharply pointed, are at present in use in these holders, and the tension is set such that the point does not scratch soft lead foil when attached to the drum.

These remarks regarding the stylus apply to the *Daily Mirror* machines, a somewhat different arrangement being employed by Professor Korn. The mechanism of the stylus is, however, a matter of the greatest importance, as is also the shape of its point and the angle that it makes with the surface of the drum.

The sparking at the point of contact of stylus with copper foil sketch may be almost overcome by shunting across it a condenser of about 1 to 1·5 microfarad capacity; the extent of sparking is probably dependent to some extent on the self-induction of the line and may not therefore be always equal. Sodium sulphate cells have been used by Korn with great success also.

A battery of from 30 to 60 volts is usually employed at the sending station, and the amount of current received at London from Paris averages between 6 and 12 milliampères; from Manchester between 9 and 18 milliampères.

The function of the transmitter is clearly to send an electric current to the receiver, which is broken constantly, the duration of the brakes depending on the width of the shellac lines of which the sketch

is constituted. We shall now see how this intermittent current is utilised to form a photographic
image in the receiving apparatus.

Fig. 31 gives a diagrammatic representation of
the sending and receiving stations. At the former
we have the drum D and stylus S and the battery B.
At the receiving station we have a drum D_1 half the
size of the transmitting drum, so that the received

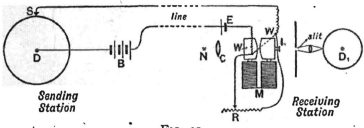

FIG. 31.

picture is one-quarter the size of the sketch transmitted. This drum revolves in a light-tight box,
and is fitted with a steel shaft cut with a screw
thread 100 to the inch, or about four to the
millimetre. The shaft turns in a fixed nut, so that
a lateral motion is given to the revolving drum,
its motion thus corresponding precisely to that of
the transmitting cylinder. A sliding lens is fitted
in the centre of the front of the " dark box," and
in front of it is placed an ebonite screen, with an
adjustable slit fitted centrally and opposite the lens.
Any light passing through the slit is focussed by
the lens as a small spot of light on D_1, and if the slit

F 2

were always illuminated by a constant amount of light, a sensitive photographic film wrapped round the drum D_1 would receive a long, thin, spiral line of exposure.

Now, however, imagine a line drawn from the centre of the filament of the Nernst lamp N to the slit, this line produced coinciding with the optic axis of the small sliding lens in the dark box. A condensing lens C projects the light from N upon the ebonite screen in which the slit is fitted.

The light passes through holes bored in the pole-pieces of a powerful electro-magnet M, across the field of which is stretched a single flat silver wire WW, and the shadow of this wire is thrown sharply over the slit, the adjustment being carried out by means of the sliding lens L. The magnet is excited by 110 volts 1 ampère from a battery of secondary cells, and the current from the connecting telephone line is passed through WW.

When current flows, this wire is laterally displaced, and consequently its shadow rises above the slit and allows the light from N to reach the sensitive film on D_1. Should the current received be more than is required just to uncover the slit, the necessary amount of extra resistance may be inserted in series with the line.

A small battery opposing the line current may be inserted at E as shown, and a regulating resistance R shunted across the galvanometer. By means of the latter the movement of the wire WW can be readily controlled, for if the line resistance be w_1 and the resistance at R be w_2, then the ratio of the current entering the " string " WW to that absorbed by the shunted resistance will be $\frac{w_2}{w_1}$. In considering displacements of the string which are very small compared with its length, we may regard the displacement as proportional to the current. Hence, by varying w_2, w_1 remaining constant, the displacement can either be regulated to work with a slit of any desired width or to accommodate a current received of any strength, the width of slit remaining constant.

In much of the work the battery E was put in series with the resistance R, so that current flowed continuously through the string and gave it a displacement opposite in direction to that caused by the line current. This procedure conduces to " dead-beatness," and it brings the string back to the zero position very rapidly the moment the line current is interrupted. The ratio of the " reverse " current to the " line " current is best varied to suit the circumstances, but if the latter be fairly uniform, the most desirable plan from the operator's point of view is to keep E and R constant, and to adjust the movement in the string caused by the line current by means of a regulating resistance in series with the line.

The currents transmitted by this system being considerably greater than those practicable with the selenium apparatus a somewhat different system of synchronising the two instruments is required. It becomes necessary, in fact, to reverse the direction of the current at the moment of synchronising. The drum of the receiving apparatus is revolved about 1 per cent. faster than the transmitting drum, and finishes its revolution rather before the trans-

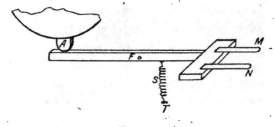

FIG. 32.

mitter, as in the case of the selenium machines. When the turn is completed the drum is checked by a metal stop, and the galvanometer circuit automatically thrown out, a relay circuit being switched in in its place. The transmitting drum on completing its turn causes a fleeting contact to be made in the reverse direction to that of the line current, and this actuates the relay, which, being polarised, is only sensitive to current in the one direction. The relay closes the local circuit which removes the check by means of an electro-magnet, and both drums therefore start off on a fresh revolution in unison.

The reverser is of various forms, and is, of course, used in most electrical instruments which require similar synchronisation. One pattern of it is seen in Fig. 32. Here, M, N are two steel tongues with platinum contacts attached to a bar which can rotate about a fulcrum F ; it is held in position by a spring S, the end of which is attached

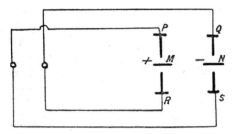

FIG. 33.

to a point T, in this case in the bed-plate. A represents a projecting pin on the cylinder or drum, which, in the position shown, depresses the end of the bar and consequently causes the tongues M, N to rise. As soon as the drum has travelled a little further round, the pin A is out of the way, hence the spring S pulls the tongues M, N down again into their normal position.

The next diagram (Fig. 33) represents the reversing arrangement. M, N are again the tongues, while P, Q and R, S are four platinum contact pins.

In the normal position of the springs they press against the pins R, S, which are connected in the manner shown to the terminals of the "line." When the synchronising pin comes into contact with the bar the tongues are raised into close contact with the pins P, Q, so that clearly the polarity at the line terminals is reversed. P, Q are the receiving circuit relay pins of the transmitter, while R, S are for the galvanometer circuit.

Towards the end of the year 1908 Professor Korn installed one of his telautographs at the offices of *L'Illustration* in Paris, another being at the *Lokal Anzeiger* offices in Berlin, under the supervision of his colleague, Dr. Glatzel, and a sketch was transmitted with considerable success, the subject being that of an aeroplane flight. The subject was topical, and the picture was published the following morning in *Le Matin*, with an article, descriptive of the event, entitled "Prodigious." And considering the fact that a complicated news picture had been wired some 800 miles in ten minutes, that would have taken several hours to come by train, for the first time in history, the enthusiasm of the *Matin* was certainly justified. I arrived in Paris the following morning and saw large crowds of people looking at the photographic print, which was displayed in the way customary with the *Matin* in their windows facing the Boulevarde. A few days later a telautograph was being constructed by Mr. Sanger Shepherd for the *Daily Mirror*, and every effort was made to finish it in time for the King's visit in January, 1909, to Berlin. Pictures were wired from Berlin to Paris of His Majesty driving through the streets of Berlin, and from those further pictures were prepared by M. Chatenet, which he attempted to re-transmit from Paris to London. But the London telautograph had only been tested a day or two previously, and was not in anything approaching good adjustment, and the results were not good enough for publication. This was after attempting the transmissions from about 1 A.M. to 3 A.M. Results soon began to come through with regularity, however, and the telautograph became a useful means of obtaining news pictures from the Continent.

An interesting break in the telautograph transmissions was caused by the great Postal strike in France, which was at its worst during the *summer* of 1909. The pressure on the telephone lines was very great at this time, as so much correspondence was carried on by means of the telephone, and it was only occasionally that the Post Office was able to spare a line for the photo-telegraphic work. On one occasion a picture was being transmitted, and the adjustments had taken a minute or two longer than usual ; the line could only be spared for about fifteen minutes, and when this time had elapsed the officials were obliged to cut our line. The picture was only about two-thirds transmitted, and the result was that the photograph was only received in part ; needless to say, the more important part of the subject was missing, and the result was quite useless for publication.

Experiments were carried out between Berlin and Paris, using one line only and an earth " return " ; the current received in this way was about 5 milli-ampères, and sufficient to work the apparatus satisfactorily.

A second English telautograph was begun in February, and an effort was made to have it ready and installed at Manchester in time to telegraph down to London the finish of the Grand National race at Aintree in March. A change was made at the same time in Manchester, the photo-telegraphic installation being removed from the office of the *Manchester Courier* to a new office specially equipped for the work. A few days before the race took place the new telautograph was taken to Manchester, and through the courtesy of the Post Office officials there a trunk line was put in and tested just in time to enable one experimental picture to be wired through. The finish of the race was taken by a press photographer, and the plate taken by a *Daily Mirror* motor car to the station at Aintree, and brought thence by train to Manchester. It was then developed and a fish-glue print of the picture was prepared and at once wired to London.

Such instances as this show how by means of photo-telegraphy a newspaper can publish a picture of some event a clear day before another paper. A few critics are still sceptical, and say : " Would not the public prefer to wait the extra day and have

Fig. 34.—Reception to Sven Hedin, wired from Paris to London by Telautograph.

a better picture—the original?" The answer is : " No." Just as the public prefer to have a brief telegram about an important event rather than wait another day for the full report, so they prefer to have a graphic representation, *i.e.*, a photograph, immediately. The advantage to the *Daily Mirror* of having interesting pictures by wire before any other paper is, in fact, obvious. During the great trial of Madame Steinheil photographs that had been taken in court late in the afternoon were telegraphed to London soon after 7 o'clock. The time of preparation of the photographs is, of course, a factor of importance ; in the earlier days it was customary for an artist to draw a line sketch of the photograph to be telegraphed, and this sketch was then copied in the camera, and a fish-glue print made from the negative on copper foil. But various improvements in the apparatus have gradually rendered possible the transmission of half-tone photographs, and thus the work of the artist is done away with, together with his time.

The preparation of these half-tone photographs will be more fully considered in the chapter dealing with the telectrograph, but mention may here be made of the work done by M. Chatenet, which has helped considerably in determining the best means of producing them.

The progress in transmission has been due, as stated above, to continual small improvements in the apparatus. The galvanometer is the most delicate, as well as the most vital, part of the instrument, and it is the greater perfection of the moving part of the galvanometer that has contributed to the improved nature of the results.

A very small period is necessary in the " string," and its weight must be very small and its strength comparatively great. A flat silver string appears to be more rapid than any form of phosphor-

Fig. 35.—Example of Fashion Plate wired by the Korn Telautograph.

bronze, and the length of it free to swing is usually about 5 cm. An improvement introduced recently

by Professor Korn is to have a flat string slightly
twisted, and the most recent galvanometers have
been provided with a collar, which can be turned
through a small angle, and this has a micrometer
scale to it, so that the angle through which the
ribbon is twisted can be accurately determined.

By using a wide slit in front of the receiving
box so that more light is admitted to the receiving
drum, with a consequent larger movement of the
shadow of the ribbon or string, it is possible to
receive the picture direct on photographic paper.
This is important, as it saves one operation in the
photographic work, and a minute or two frequently decides whether a picture can be " got
in " an early edition of the paper or not.

The inertia of the photographic sensitive film
plays an interesting part in the more brilliant
results obtained direct on sensitive paper. When
the wider slit is used the tension of the galvanometer string is made less so that the shadow
will rise to the necessary extent to quite open
the slit. As it rises and falls each time there
is a current sent through the string, the light
is obviously greatest at the moment when the
slit is totally uncovered and is least at the two
instants when the slit is just a little opened and
nearly closed. Now before light can produce a
developable effect in a photographic film it has to
overcome the chemical inertia of the film, and unless

it be of sufficient intensity to do this, nothing is
obtained on development. The result is that if the
complete upward and backward displacement of
the string takes a time T, and during that time
the sensitive film on the revolving drum is travelling with a velocity v, the length of the mark
produced on development will not be vT, but
will be vt, where $t < T$ and the distance v (T−t)

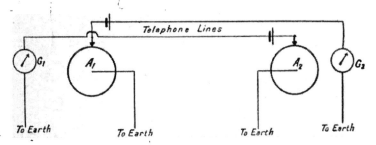

FIG. 36.

corresponds to the inertia of the film. Consequently the darkest parts only of the component
dots of the picture are given in the developed print,
and there is more·contrast in the picture.

Simultaneous transmissions in two directions
have been recently suggested by Professor Korn,
which would reduce the cost of photo-telegraphy,
and save operators' time as well. The scheme is
seen at a glance in Fig. 36. The parallel lines
represent the telephone lines between the two
stations. , A_1 is the transmitting drum of one
machine, G_1 the string galvanometer; A_2 and G_2

are the similar parts of the other instrument. One wire of the telephone line is used in each case for the return, the current flowing through the earth. This method has not so far been practically tested, but will doubtless be useful when a greater number of photographs are transmitted.

The question of the greatest possible length of transmission by the telautograph is daily becoming more important. In 1908 an experiment was made with Korn's selenium machines between Berlin and London, the two lines Berlin-Paris and Paris-London being joined at Paris by M. Chatenet, who acted as " intermediary." This was necessary owing to the impossibility of speaking clearly from Berlin to London ; anything spoken had therefore to be said to the Paris operator, who " passed it on " to the Berlin operator, and *vice versâ*. Then, when the adjustments were made, the Paris operator simply connected up the Berlin-Paris and Paris-London lines on his switchboard.

These experiments were, as already stated, carried out with the selenium apparatus, and the current received at London, about 0·25 milliampère, was insufficient to work with. The stronger current for the synchronising was sufficient to work the relay, however, and as it is of the same magnitude as the galvanometer current used in the telautograph there is little doubt but that the latter instrument could be worked effectually between

Berlin and London, and probably over distances up to 1,500 miles.

FIG. 37.—Line drawing transmitted by Telautograph.

Beyond this stage it would be necessary to have a more sensitive relay for the synchronising, and a more sensitive galvanometer. The latter is as easy

P.T.   G

of accomplishment as the former. The silver string in the galvanometer can be made finer ; I have obtained them in this country less than $\frac{1}{2000}$th inch in diameter, while by using the silvered quartz threads suggested by Duddell for the Einthoven galvanometer a thread $\frac{1}{12000}$th inch diameter can be employed. The magnetic field can also be greatly increased by building the magnets considerably larger and making the windings take enough current for complete saturation of the iron. The instrument then becomes exceedingly sensitive, and it merely remains for the optical parts to be suitably constructed.

As explained elsewhere, the string of the galvanometer should have a period which is neither equal to nor a multiple nor sub-multiple of the period of the interruptions due to the transmitting apparatus ; this applies only to the transmission of half-tone line photographs, which consist of a definite number of lines per unit of length. The natural period of the string can be varied in several ways. It can most readily be measured by means of the recording apparatus described in Chapter V. If a short current be sent through the string by means of suddenly tapping a Morse key, a jerk is given to it and it is displaced through a distance d (at the centre). It then swings back to zero and then past the zero point, to a point distant $d - x$ from it where $d - x$ is less than d. One has, in fact, a damped oscillation, and the string does not actually come to rest for a definite time. During this time t

Fig. 38.—Example of line sketch from photograph, wired by the Korn Telautograph from Paris to London.

there may be n complete vibrations, from which the natural period t/n can be ascertained. If the string be made to cast a shadow over an illuminated slit through which the light passes when it is

G 2

displaced, and this light fall on a rapidly travelling band of photographic film, and a tap be then given with the Morse key as above described, a·record of the movements of the string is obtained. If the rate at which the film travels be known, it is easy to calculate the period of the galvanometer.

.The string has a shorter period if its length be shortened or its tension increased, and the damping of its oscillations can be effectually increased if a twist be given to one end of it in the manner already indicated. The effect of damping can be seen if we consider the equation of the movement of the string, which is of the form

$$d = ae^{-kt} \cos (nt + a),$$

where d is the displacement; ae^{-kt} decreases as t increases; k is the damping constant, and e^{-kt} the damping factor. K has got to be as large as possible, and can be made large if we increase the friction at the ends of the string. Suppose the string to be displaced still through the distance d, where f is the elastic force, the work done is df; this is the measure of the potential energy of the centre of the string, provided we subtract l, the loss of energy through heating owing to the friction; l increases as f is increased, while d is diminished for the same amount of current sent through the string.

The rapidity of damping is readily seen from the diagram shown in Fig. 39, which is drawn to scale

from an actual photographic record of a short
current sent through the galvanometer.

Returning now to the question of possible distance of transmission, it is clear that for a very
sensitive galvanometer the displacement for the
same current would require to be much greater ;
the period would be lengthened, f and l diminished, and the rate of working diminished also ;
with a silvered quartz fibre, the period would be
much longer than that of the flat silver ribbon now

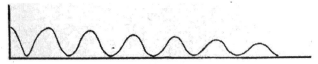

FIG. 39.—Damping of oscillograph string. The ordinates
represent the displacement, d.

in use, and the transmission would therefore be of
an altogether slower nature. The capacity of a
long line would be correspondingly higher, and
this would again necessitate slowness in the transmission.

The theoretical limits of distance of transmission
are fairly wide, but the practical limits are unfortunately very different. Yet such distances as those
between London and Rome, London and Marseilles,
etc., should be by no means insuperable.

That the telautograph could be put to other uses
than that of transmitting photographs is seen
from its ability to transmit writing. Written

matter comes out very clearly in the received pic-

FIG. 40.—Example of half-tone photograph transmitted from Berlin to Paris by Telautograph.

tures, as do maps and diagrams of all kinds. In the case of typewritten matter, for which a blue or violet ink is usually employed, it is necessary to make a photographic negative, using an ortho-chromatic plate and a yellow contrast filter in front of the camera lens.   The writing then appears colourless in the negative, and hence dense " black " in the fish-glue print made from it. Type-written matter has been telegraphed successfully from Paris to London.

It will thus be seen that a signature for banking purposes could be sent by wire, the signature being written direct in the shellac ink upon a clean sheet of copper or lead foil.   This, by the way, must be scrupulously clean, and for the copper a weak solu-tion of potassium cyanide may be used with advan-tage.   Another method is to rub the metal with a cloth and some finely-powdered pumice-stone. The telegraphy of signatures for identification purposes may be an important feature of later work.

The telautograph may be said to have solved the problem of commercial photo-telegraphy, and to have directly stimulated the efforts of others who may have contributed to the development of the work, or who may be now endeavouring to con-tribute to it in the future.

CHAPTER IV.

THE THORNE - BAKER SYSTEM — DIFFERENCES BETWEEN THE TELECTROGRAPH AND EARLIER CHEMICAL SYSTEMS—ELECTROLYTIC RECORDS OF CURRENTS TRANSMITTED THROUGH LONG CABLES — THE THORNE-BAKER LINE-BALANCE—WORK WITH THE ELECTROLYTIC TELECTROGRAPH.

THE simplest and most practical apparatus for photo-telegraphy at the present time is fairly admitted to be the telectrograph, which came into use by the *Daily Mirror* in July, 1909. It was seen in the first chapter that Bakewell had obtained some promising results with his chemical telautograph, in which he used a picture produced in lines on a metal foil, the lines being of an insulating character such as offered by shellac, gum, or glue, etc.

One of his chief difficulties was found in the synchronism, yet results were obtained, and some of the most interesting of these were telegraphed *written matter*. The telectrograph, by which

name I have designated my own modification
of Bakewell's apparatus, has proved successful,
because (i.) all the mechanical parts have been
most carefully modelled on lines dictated by
innumerable failures and experiments, and (ii.) by
means of the line-balancer I have made the
receiving instrument of such a character that the
distortion, lag and line-surges met with when
working with long-distance cables can be instantly
overcome by simple regulation.

Mr. Sanger Shepherd, whose workmanship is
perhaps the most accurate and effectual of any
instrument maker in the world, undertook from
the start the constructional work, and to him
largely belongs the credit of the success of the
Daily Mirror's photo-telegraphic work. In transmitting a photograph seven inches by five, made
up of fifty lines to the inch, the Caselli
stylus has to traverse 7 × 50 or 350 lines per
revolution. With one revolution of the transmitting drum in two seconds we have 175 dots
per second recorded on the receiving paper. If
one dot were $\frac{1}{175}$th of a second later than it should
be it would fall into line with the dot of the next
line in the line photograph. The figure of merit
in synchronisation requires to be within an error
of at least 1 in 500 to obtain intelligible results.
Thus the synchronising mechanism has to be very
fairly "perfect," and it has been necessary to

make the balancing of the stylus and various other mechanical details equally precise.

If we refer to Fig. 1 (Chapter I.) we see that at the sending station we have a revolving metal drum A, to which the lead foil half-tone photograph is attached. This revolves while a stylus traces a spiral path over the picture in virtue of its being given a lateral motion. The style is fixed to an arm (Fig. 28, Chapter III.), which has screwed to it a half-nut, threaded so as to fit on the shaft F, which is also threaded. Hence as the shaft turns, between steel centres, the half-nut travels along it, and so draws the stylus along too. In the telectrograph there are 75 threads to the inch, so that the style moves laterally with a velocity of $\frac{1}{150}$th inch per second.

The style is of special design, as shown diagrammatically in Fig. 41, turning about pivots P and being provided with a tension screw T. The point of contact is a V-shaped iridium tracer I, which withstands the constant sparking caused by the makes and breaks of the current. The actual point must be very fine, yet not fine enough to scratch the lead; the tension is regulated by the screw T.

The battery, usually 100 volts, consists of secondary cells, and hence a series of currents are sent into the line exactly as in the case of Korn's telautograph. At the receiving end we have a cylinder B, the same size as A, and revolving in synchronism, its movement being controlled in the way already described and in common use in certain systems of ordinary telegraphy.

Round B is wrapped a piece of specially prepared paper, containing in its composition certain chemical substances which decompose on the passage through them of an electric current. The un-

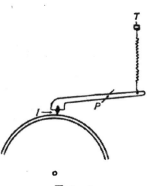

FIG. 41.

decomposed chemicals must be colourless, the decomposition products must be *coloured*. Hence, in theory, whenever a current is sent from the sending instrument it passes through the paper, *via* the stylus, and a black or coloured mark is made on the paper, the length of the mark, l, measured along the circumference, being equal to tu, where $u =$ the velocity of the surface of the drum, and t the duration of the current. When, however, the sending and receiving instruments are connected by a long distance line, instead of an ordinary resistance, we find that for a current of duration t, the length of the chemical mark is considerably greater than tu:

If we were to send one brief current from transmitting to receiving station, say of $\frac{1}{200}$th second duration, and we were to place a piece of chemically sensitive paper on the receiving drum, the latter revolving in the ordinary way, we should get a mark of this form ◐, showing that the line takes an appeciable time to charge up, and when charged, requires time again to fully discharge. This can be represented by the curve shown in Fig. 42. If we were to transmit several brief currents of equal period, and were then to stop suddenly, we should get a continuity of marking, not dying away for an appreciable time.

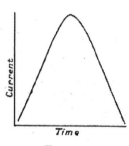

FIG. 42.

These difficulties can be almost entirely overcome by the line balance described by me in November, 1909,* in which a current with shunt capacity and an inductance to time the phase where necessary is sent into the line to damp down the secondary surges. The arrangement is seen in Fig. 43. D is the receiving drum and S a platinum stylus. The shunt circuit consists of two similar parts, a secondary cell being in each, B_1 and B_2; a variable inductance in each (not shown); and a variable resistance of 1,000 ohms, R_1 and R_2. The ends of the resist-

* Journal of the Society of Arts, 2975, 30.

ances are joined in the manner shown, while
between the sliding contacts of the resistances is a
variable capacity K ; the capacity ranges from o
to 1 microfarad.

When a photograph is received the waves sent
into the line are distorted by their passage through
it, and this distortion appears as an elongation of

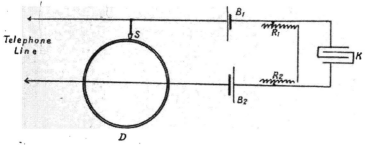

FIG. 43.

the chemical dots or marks made upon the paper
on the receiving drum as already described ; the
greater the distortion the less is the resistance
required in R_1 and R_2; the greater the capacity of
the line connecting the two machines the more the
capacity one must introduce by means of K.

It can now readily be seen how practical the
telectrograph is for commercial work. The
operator carefully watches the paper on the drum
during the first two or three revolutions, and
according as the marks are crisp or blurred he
varies the various regulating elements. Hence

before any important portion of the photograph
has been transmitted he can ensure its reception
being good. In any optical method of reception,
on the other hand, should any error have occurred
in the preliminary adjustments, the operator cannot
know of his fault until after both the reception has

FIG. 44.—1. Capacity on line. 2. No capacity. 3. Capacity
on line, but balancer in shunt.

Photograph showing the balancing effect of the Telectrograph
arrangement. Currents were sent to the receiver by
closing a circuit with a Morse key. The chemical marks
produced are elongated or "tailed" when capacity is
shunted on the line (1). They are short and end abruptly
with no capacity (2). The capacity effect is obviated by
the balancer (3).

been completed and the film or sensitive paper has
been developed. When we remember that the cost
of the telephone line between London and Paris is
four shillings for three minutes, or over a farthing
a second, the need for rapidity becomes apparent.
The machine must be simple, rapid, and, if possible, certain ; the preliminary tests and adjustments reduced to the minimum, and the operator
himself must be quick and intelligent, and be able
to locate a fault rapidly.

It is interesting to note that the distortion caused in transmission through a long line or cable is considerably lessened where there is high leakance. Heaviside has shown that in telephony the distortion D is given by the equation

$$D = \frac{R}{2\,L} - \frac{S}{2\,K},$$

and the attenuation A by

$$A = \frac{R}{2\,L} + \frac{S}{2\,K},$$

where R is resistance, L inductance, K capacity, and S leakance. When leakance is very small on a line of considerable weight we have the distortion approximately proportional to $\frac{R}{2\,L}$.

The capacity effects are thus less pronounced when there is much leakance on a line, if the latter take place at various well distributed intervals, as its effect is to obstruct the charging up of the line. Capacity does not reduce the energy transmitted along the line, but its effect, as well known in telephony, is to cause length of time in discharge; the inductance is valuable as it counteracts the distortion, but it is small in submarine and underground cables, because the current flows through the two lines, which are close together, in opposite directions, the self-induction of each being thereby largely neutralised by the other.

It is interesting to note that often during very wet weather less " balancing " of the line is required in working with the telectrograph, this bearing out the distortion expression

$$\frac{R}{2\,L} - \frac{S}{2\,K}.$$

The capacity of a single line of diameter d and length l at a height H above the ground is given by the following expression :—

$$C = \frac{l \times 2\cdot415 \times 10^6}{log_{10}\,\dfrac{4\,H}{d}},$$

but this becomes effectively much less where there are two lines close together. In the case of telephone cables we can divide the capacity of one line by two to get the total capacity of the closed line, since the capacity of two condensers in series is equal to half that of one singly. As will be seen later, the capacity of a Paris—London single line is 10·6 m.f., so that the capacity of the two lines forming a closed circuit is 5·3 m.f. The submarine cable between Sangatte (France) and St. Margaret's Bay is 5·52 m.f. in capacity, or more than equal to the total capacity of the land lines, which measure 287 miles against 23 miles of the submarine.

The preparation of the chemical paper for receiving the photographs is not an easy matter, as one must have a paper always conductive, and therefore always in a moist condition, and whilst it. is sufficiently absorbent it. must have a smooth surface, as otherwise the grain is painfully prominent when the picture is copied for reproduction. The resistance of the paper may be anything from 1,000 to 5,000 ohms, and as it must mark instantaneously with a current of about 1 milliampère it requires to be extremely sensitive. The speed at which the paper passes under the stylus is 3·75 inches per second, and since the amount of the element liberated which causes the discoloration is by weight equal to the product of current, time, and electro-chemical equivalent, it is seen that an exceedingly small amount of chemical action takes place. When much current is lost in the line it is sometimes necessary to increase the voltage at the sending end. · Although only about a milliampère of current flows actually through the paper,. twenty or thirty may flow through the line, this excess of course going into the shunt circuit or balancer of the receiver. The secondary discharge of a small induction coil is quite sufficient to mark the paper used, so that the effect of electrolysis can be produced with practically "no current," provided the tension be sufficiently high.

. The first experiments were made with the telectrograph in 1909 at the Imperial International

Exhibition, Shepherd's Bush, where demonstrations were given about eight times daily, photographs being telegraphed from one machine to the other through an artificial " line " of about 2,000

Fig. 45.—Portrait of first lady councillor of Liverpool. Wired by the Telectrograph from Manchester to London.

Ω resistance; the machines stood some 16 or 20 feet apart, so that both sending and receiving operations could be readily observed together.

The method of synchronising was practically the same as that described for the telautograph, except in 'so far as the receiving machine was concerned. The " line " terminals were connected to the spring tongues of the reverser (see Chapter III.), which was in contact with two upper platinum pins during nearly the whole revolution, these pins leading one to the stylus and the other to the drum, *i.e.*, the back of the sensitive paper.   At synchronism the check which stopped the drum revolving temporarily automatically lowered the tongues into contact with two other pins which led directly to the polarised relay, the latter switching in the mechanism for withdrawing the check.

The machines worked so satisfactorily over the artificial line that in July, 1909, I was tempted to place a similar instrument in Manchester, where an installation of Professor Korn's apparatus was in full swing, as already described.   The first experiments over this line, some 200 miles in length, were very disappointing.   The attempts were made with line sketches, not half-tone photographs, and the lines appeared on the paper as so many smudges ; each mark had a long tail, and it was evident that secondary discharges were coming from the line into the paper. These discharges were much more noticeable some days than others.

It thus became obvious that the capacity and induction effects would have to be counterbalanced, and after a series of experiments the means already described were adopted, with what success has been

seen from the quality of the pictures telegraphed
with this instrument since published in the *Daily Mirror*.

It has already been explained that a graduation
of tone in a photograph is represented in a line half-tone photograph by lines becoming gradually narrower. This tapering down of the width of the lines in the telegraphed picture received is wonderfully reproduced, and the results are therefore truly "photographic"; indeed, examined a short distance away, they are, if the synchronisation has been good, hardly distinguishable from the original photographs.

FIG. 46.—Portrait of Mr. Howarth, telegraphed from Manchester to London by the Thorne-Baker Telectrograph.

In October, 1909, a telectrograph was installed in Paris, but here again trouble was at first experienced. In the first place, the line is half as long again as the London-Manchester line, and in the second, its various elements are distinctly different. The first picture received was successful, but then the line conditions must have changed, because for several days the results were extremely bad, each

Receiving a photograph on the Telectrograph.

Opposite p. 100.

dot running into next, so that the whole surface of the paper was discoloured and all the details of the image hopelessly intermingled. I then increased the capacity of the condenser in the line balancer, and the photographs were also temporarily made with a coarse line screen (30 to the inch), and the quality was at once better. A great deal depends, needless to say, on the quality of the half-tone photographs, which require quite a particular method of preparation.

The method of making these photographs is as follows : The picture to be telegraphed is pinned flat to a board or placed in a frame with glass over it, and fixed vertically in a copying apparatus. It is usually illuminated with an arc lamp at either side with reflectors. The camera used for copying it has a half-tone screen fixed at a certain distance in front of the sensitive plate. This screen consists of a glass plate ruled with a certain number of lines to the inch ; thirty or thirty-five lines to the inch is known as a " coarse " screen, the number for high-class illustrations, printed on surfaced paper, being 120 upwards to the inch. Usually two such screens are used, crossed so that the rulings are at an angle of 90° to each other, and then the picture is broken up into dots ; but it can easily be seen that where the picture is put on a cylinder and travels round beneath a tracing point, lines are preferable to dots ; the lines of course lie along the length of the cylinder, so that the tracer scrapes over them and not along them.   In the case of dots the tracer would go in between two adjacent ones very often, or, as its path is at a slight angle .

Fig. 47.—Half-tone single line negative image, as ordinarily used for the Telectrograph.

to the path of a fixed point on the circumference of the cylinder, it would occasionally touch two dots in consecutive lines at once, and interference would be caused.

The single-line screen has the effect of breaking

up the picture into parallel lines which vary in width according to the density of the photograph at each point. Thus, in the case of a portrait, the dark coat would be represented by wide lines close together, a light part of the face by fine lines correspondingly wide apart, the distance between the *centre* of any two lines being always constant. If there are fifty lines per inch, no line can be wider than $\frac{1}{50}$ inch; as a matter of fact, it should not be wider than $\frac{1}{50} - t$, where t is the width of the point of the stylus, otherwise a dark part of the picture would appear in the telegraph as a " dead black." The *print* from the half-tone negative is now prepared by printing from it (in arc light) upon a sheet of thick lead foil coated with a thin layer of fish-glue rendered sensitive to light by means of a soluble bichromate. When printed it is held under a tap, and all the unexposed parts dissolve away, *i.e.*, the parts in between the lines. The print is now dried and placed between two polished steel plates, and put into a press. This causes the glue image to sink into the soft metal without distorting it, and a smooth commutator surface is obtained, which therefore offers no resistance to the stylus, while it allows of very intimate contact between the stylus and the picture.

The image is made *negative* for the telectrograph, as wherever there is bare metal a black mark is produced at the receiving instrument. The image is made visible by staining up the print in an aniline dye solution, the glue taking up the colour readily.

Photo-engravers know that in making a half-tone photograph, even with the cross screen, a good deal of the detail is lost, and this is only natural when we consider that, instead of a solid black or grey, we have only dots on a white ground. In

Fig. 48.—Finish of the St. Leger, wired by the Telectrograph.

making a single-line picture a great deal more is lost, and thus before making the screen negative the original has to be considerably retouched, the contours have to be very clearly defined and accentuated, and the paler tints have to be made considerably bolder, as these lose the most in the reproduction. The solid blacks, on the other hand, require to be made *grey*, so that the lines representing them in the half-tone picture are not too wide and close together.

Future progress rests so much on greater perfection being obtained in the line pictures that I have dwelt at some length on these points. The present systems are good and practicable ; it is perfection of detail that is required. · M. Chatenet is a particularly clever photo-engraver, and has rendered much assistance in finding the best means of the preparation of the half-tone pictures. A considerable time elapsed at Manchester before the photo-engravers there were able to make really suitable line prints ; but, having once found out the " right way," the work proceeds quite smoothly. But what I would like to point out is that, although telegraphed pictures are now to be seen so regularly in the *Daily Mirror* that they occasion no surprise, they have only become what they are through the attention from start to finish given to minute details.

By means of the apparatus described in Chapter VI. it has become possible to make a great variety of experiments, transmitting pictures over an artificial telephone line in which resistance, self-induction, leakance, and capacity can be varied at will. By examining oscillographic records of these transmissions, various arrangements for overcoming line faults can be tested, and their practical utility estimated. The problem of photo-telegraphy over telephone lines is closely allied in many respects to ordinary telephone work, only that the electrical impulses are of far longer duration, and represent small parts of a picture instead of vocal sounds.

As the function of the transmitting instrument is merely that of an interrupter, it is clear that the sending battery can be included in the receiving station, hence a portable apparatus is not impossible. Portable instruments are now, as a matter of fact, being constructed, in which the motive power is derived from a particular form of clockwork mechanism. The portable machine is the key to general commercial utility, and its developments will be watched with interest.

FIG. 49.—M. Riolle, Public Prosecutor in the Steinheil case; wired from Paris to London by the Thorne - Baker Telectrograph.

One drawback to the telectrograph, viz., that a negative image had to be used on the transmitting cylinder instead of a positive (the latter being more easily and rapidly prepared), has recently been overcome. A positive print having about fifty lines to the inch is used, and at the receiver a current is passed through the electrolytic paper which continuously discolours it. The currents transmitted

from the sending machine are of opposite direction
to this continuous current, and neutralise it. Hence,
whenever the stylus of the transmitter sends a
current through the line it neutralises the continuous current, and so prevents the latter from
making an electrolytic dot. As soon as the transmitter current has ceased, it is immediately wiped

Fig. 50.—News photograph wired from Manchester to London
of a railway accident at Stalybridge.

out by the continuous current, which is of course
shunted on to the telephone line.

The use of a double current system in telegraphy
is well known, and greatly increases the possible
rate of working, as it hastens the ordinarily slow
discharge of the line. It thus becomes possible
to work with finer screens in preparing the photographs, and to obtain a correspondingly greater
amount of detail.

CHAPTER V.

CONSIDERATIONS OF THE TELEPHONE AND TELEGRAPH LINES AND THEIR INFLUENCE ON PHOTO-TELEGRAPHY.

As the two qualities, leakance and resistance, of the lines connecting two photo-telegraphic instruments have a final influence on the limits of long-distance transmissions, and the capacity and inductance factors have a large influence on the quality of the pictures and the rate, etc., with which they can be transmitted, some short discussion of the matter becomes necessary.

The actual effect of capacity is, as has been pointed out elsewhere, a lengthening of the duration of the current, but we shall now see how these effects can be experimentally demonstrated. A modified form of the Einthoven, or string galvanometer, was employed to record photographically the effects of capacity on the currents transmitted through a high-resistance line by the transmitter, as used in the telautograph and telectrograph. The arrangement is seen in Fig. 51. A band of sensitive film MOQ travels over rollers in a light-tight box, being actuated by a well-regulated clockwork motor ; one or two strings (silver wires $\frac{1}{1000}$th inch thick) are free to move laterally between the tunnelled poles of the electro-magnet, and a shutter is attached to them where the optic axis meets them. N is a Nernst lamp, and L a lens. The lens in the tube T throws a real image of the shutter over the horizontal slit S. The terminals A, B of the galvanometer strings are connected to the metal drum and stylus of a photo-telegraphic

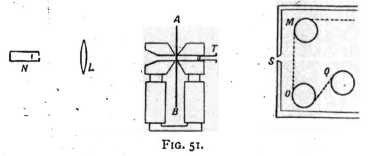

FIG. 51.

transmitter, across which capacity can be shunted, or inductance, etc., can be placed in the circuit.

Every time the stylus of the transmitter comes in contact with the metal, current flows through AB, which is laterally displaced ; hence the shutter uncovers the slit S more or less according to the current strength. A series of images of the slit is thus seen on the moving film MOQ on development. The elongation and widening of the image due to capacity can be seen clearly on comparing the two records shown in Figs. 52 and 53.

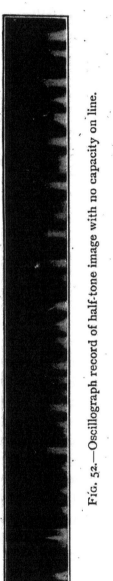

FIG. 52.—Oscillograph record of half-tone image with no capacity on line.

FIG. 53.—The same with capacity, showing the elongation and widening of the "teeth."

These oscillographic records show many things of great interest. Firstly, that if the metallic space between each of several consecutive glue lines in a half-tone print be s, greater than that s_1 between each line in another print, the current passing through the strings A, B is greater in the case of the s lines than in that of the s_1, although the line resistance, battery power, etc., be the same in both cases; hence a definite time is required for the current transmitted to reach a maximum value, the possible value not being so nearly reached when the interruptions are very rapid as when slower, and the maximum value being very rarely reached. Secondly, that where a large number of consecutive currents of equal period p are transmitted, the displacement of the galvanometer strings increases gradually to a maximum value, then decreases, and so on, instead of remaining always equal and proportional to p. Thirdly, that when the period p has a certain value, equal to the natural period of swing of the strings, the displacement is excessive, and very much higher than that obtainable under any other circumstances, R and C remaining equal.

The effect of a number of currents of equal period to cause a gradual extension of the swings which reach a maximum and then decrease, indicates that a dead-beat action like the electrolytic one is preferable to any form of moving part, where there is definite momentum, and kinetic energy.

The overhead wires of the Paris-London tele-phone line are 600 lbs. copper wire in France and 400 lbs. (per mile) in England. Their capacities and resistances are as follows:—

	Length in miles.	Resistance in ohms.	Capacity of each wire in micro-farads.
London to St. Margaret's Bay	84·5	183	1·32
St. Margaret's Bay to Sangatte (cable).	23·0	143	5·52
Sangatte to Paris . . .	199·0	294	3·33
Paris (underground) . .	4·8	70	0·43
	311·3	690	10·60

The total capacity is thus 5·30 microfarads, and the resistance 1,380 Ω.

In the lines from Manchester to London there are lines of different weights, from 300 lbs. to 600 lbs. per mile. The "standard cable" employed as a unit consists of an air-space paper cable with a loop resistance of 88 ohms per mile, and an average mutual electrostatic capacity of ·054 microfarad per mile between wire and wire of one pair. The 300 lbs. overhead wire may be said to be about eleven times as efficient per mile for telephone work as the standard cable, the 600 lbs. line about sixteen times. The wire to wire capacity of the overhead lines (300 lbs.)

is ·00918 microfarad, the capacity of a wire to earth ·0153 per mile.

If we compare a mile of the submarine cable with a mile of the overhead as above, the capacities are roughly as 0·24 to ·0245; and there being twenty-three miles of cable in the Paris-London line, it will be seen that the difficulties of working over it are considerably greater than those experienced in our own country.

In the case of an alternating current passing through the lines, there is a definite attenuation factor according to Pupin $= e^{-\beta m}$, where e is the base of Naperian logarithms, β the attenuation *constant*, and m the mileage. β is the fraction of the current at any moment lost in the passage of that current through a mile of line. The current employed in the telectrograph is, as already explained, of a character somewhat comparable with an alternating current, but with a continuous current impressed on it. How far these figures are applicable to the photo-telegraphic work remains to be found; the contrary current used in the telectrograph is especially a "wipe-out" current, and prevents the latter part of each cable discharge.

The practical effect of the line capacity is to lengthen the time during which a discharge takes place in the receiving apparatus. Thus if one very brief current be sent through a high-capacity line to the receiver—an ideal oscillograph absolutely

P.T.   I

dead beat, for example—the action would be longer in time than the duration of closing of the circuit at the transmitting end.

The records made with the recording apparatus already described show that when currents are transmitted through a line with considerable capacity the " teeth " widen, and are inclined one to run into the next.   This effect is in accordance with the results obtained on the telectrograph, which forms a useful and very sensitive recording apparatus in itself.   When a series of short contacts are made on the transmitter these should produce short marks at the receiver, but the actual effect is that one mark runs into the next.

What is required, then, in an ideal system is the shortening up of these elongated impulses, so that the effect in the receiver for current of duration t is also of duration t.   This result is obtained to a very fair extent in the balancer already described in the chapter dealing with the telectrograph.

· The reader may possibly have thought that the introduction of the above matter was needless in treating the subject of photo-telegraphy, but the leakance of long-distance lines and their capacity, and the attenuation factor, are the three things which chiefly decide the question : How far and how quickly can photographs be telegraphed ?

The receiving apparatus destined for the best work between two places A and B is usually of a different character from that suitable for two other places C and D.   In extending our work and covering very great distances we must build the apparatus to suit the conditions under which it is to be used.

CHAPTER VI.

THE TELESTEREOGRAPH OF M. BELIN—THE
EARLY WORK OF BELIN—CHANGES IN HIS
SYSTEM—RECENT EXPERIMENTS.

ONE of the most indefatigable workers in the
field of photo-telegraphy is M. Edouard Belin, who
has been for some years actively engaged in working out a system of his own. His apparatus has
been designated the telestereograph, but as his
method of transmission has quite recently under-
gone a radical change, it will be better to describe
his first successful models by themselves.

The use of a relief photograph, in which different
tones in the image are represented by different
thicknesses of the film, to vary the amount of
resistance in an electric circuit containing a suitable receiver, has been referred to in the intro-
ductory chapter, and the idea is a very old one.
But the methods employed by Belin, both in the
mechanism for varying the resistance and in the
means of reception, were very ingenious, and he
obtained some promising results over artificial lines
and loop telephone lines, which unfortunately never
seemed to surpass a definite standard attained in
1908.

A photograph in relief is obtained by printing
from an ordinary negative upon what is termed
carbon tissue, this being paper coated with gelatine,
which is rendered sensitive to light by the addition
of a bichromate. When sufficiently exposed, the
paper is " developed " in hot water, when the
gelatine washes away from the unexposed parts, but
remains insoluble where there has been much
exposure ; moreover, in the " half-tones," the
gelatine washes away only to an extent depending
on the amount of exposure, *i.e.*, on the density of

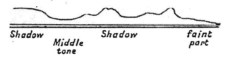

Shadow   Shadow   faint
      Middle   part
      tone

FIG. 54.

the negative. The relief picture, if we were to
cut a fine section transversely through the film,
would therefore appear as shown in Fig. 54.

Now let us suppose such a relief picture wrapped
round the drum D_1 (Fig. 55) of Belin's transmitter.
This is a heavy metal drum turning between centres,
the whole drum, etc., moving laterally so that a
stylus fixed at S traces a spiral path over the photograph. Now this stylus consists in reality of a
sapphire or a hardened steel point fitted to the end
of a rod attached to a long arm movable about F,
the fulcrum. The diagram is not drawn to scale,
S being actually close to the fulcrum. When a

high relief in the photograph happens to be at the point S the stylus is pressed outwards an amount d, so that the small platinum wheel W fixed at the end of this arm is displaced an amount $d \times M$, if the distance from F to R be M times as great as that from S to F.

The movement to and fro of this little wheel is therefore always in accordance with the relief of

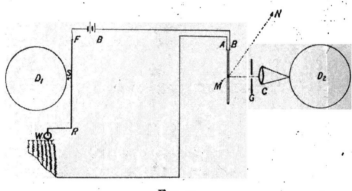

FIG. 55.

the photograph. It travels over a very small rheostat, consisting of several coils of different resistances, one end of each coil being soldered to a thin copper plate, the other end to one unit of the telephone line. These copper strips are each separated by a narrow strip of insulating material, and the top surface worked dead flat, so that the wheel W travels backwards and forwards over them; the surface of this rheostat should in reality lie along the circumference of a circle whose centre is F and radius FW.

The top of the metal arm FR is joined to the other wire of the telephone line ; the function of the Belin transmitter is thus to send into the line a practically continuous current which varies in intensity owing to the wheel W being in contact with a resistance coil whose resistance is in accord with the amount of relief at each instant at the stylus S.

This varying current (continuous because the rheostat strips are so close together that the wheel is always in contact with two or more adjacent strips) is utilised at the receiving station to form a photographic image.

For this purpose Belin employs an oscillograph of the Blondel pattern, which consists of two fine wires stretched across the field of a fairly powerful electro-magnet. The current passes down one string and up the other, not through both in the same direction as in the case of Korn's string shutter galvanometer ; hence, owing to the torque produced, the wires (AB in the figure) twist the small mirror M attached to them at the centre.

To make the damping factor e^{-kt} as great as possible, the moving part works in oil, but though this damps down the vibrations set up owing to the inflow of a sudden current, it must necessarily reduce the sensitiveness. This reduced sensitiveness is not of great consequence, because the change in intensity of the current is not very rapid nor periodic as it is in the case of the transmission of a single-line half-tone photograph. But it renders the obtaining of very fine details uncertain, one merging into the other or being lost altogether. It is of course possible to increase the sensitiveness of the galvanometer by using a more powerful magnetic field, and by using longer wires, but where oil is used in the latter case there would be more friction owing to increased field of surface tension, and I think that eventually M. Belin will be obliged to utilise the methods of damping the vibrations that have been applied to the string galvanometer in place of oil.

Now let us see how the photographic image is formed. A Nernst lamp N (Fig. 55) is placed at such a position that a pencil of light concentrated from it upon the mirror M is reflected upon a diaphragm G. This diaphragm has a rectangular aperture, so that the light reflected from M on to it when M is in the zero position falls upon one end of the aperture; as the mirror swings to one side, so the light falls more towards the other end of the aperture, etc. Now this aperture, which had much better have been a triangular one as Korn uses in his selenium machines, is covered with a graduated sheet of glass, which Belin terms his "scale of tints." It is merely a photographic negative having practically no silver deposition at one end of the rectangle, and graduating to a dense deposit at the other end. As the mirror swings to one side, so the light from it falls on a denser portion of the. scale of tints, and less light emerges from the glass.

Behind the diaphragm is a condenser C, which refracts the collected light and brings it to a point on the. drum D_2, round which a sensitive film is wrapped. The intensity of this spot of ·light is proportional to the current, hence inversely to the relief in the photograph. The drum D_2 travels sideways as it revolves, the pitch of thread used being the same as that in the transmitter. It travels in a light-tight box fitted with a tube and diaphragm, as in the case of the telautograph. But M. Belin has happily arranged that the one cylinder serves both as transmitter and receiver.

In 1907 and 1908 Belin made various experiments over a long-distance telephone line, with the two apparatus in one room under observation. Thus he had two lines between Paris and Lyons linked up at Lyons, the two machines being at Paris, and the. current had therefore to travel to Lyons and back while passing from the transmitter to the receiver.

His method of ,synchronising differs little from that already described, but in the most recent models he has arranged that the cylinders may be driven at one of three different speeds, so that the transmission can be effected rapidly or slowly as desired. This is a very useful feature for experimental instruments.

.The method of employing a rheostat and travelling wheel has now been more or less abandoned, and he has adapted to the instruments a special form of microphone, which has given some remarkably good results over artificial lines, *i.e.*, under laboratory conditions.

It is of course well known that if a diaphragm of iron be fixed near the poles of a magnet, the magnetic lines of force pass through the diaphragm. If the diaphragm be brought nearer to or further from the poles, a change in the magnetic field takes place. If small coils be wound round the pole-pieces and connected in series with each other and with a battery and telephone, then any shift in the position of the diaphragm will be noticed by a sound in the telephone. Belin conceived the idea of making the stylus press against the diaphragm of the microphone, so that the pressure on it would vary in accordance with the relief in the photographic image ; this would vary the magnetic field and so change the power of a current of electricity passed through the microphone in series with a battery and the two wires of the Blondel oscillograph.

It will at once be seen that in this procedure we are dealing with currents of very low magnitudes, and Belin found that considerable modification of his apparatus was necessary. In the first place the relief in the photographs as used for his original machines was much too great, and whereas very thickly-coated tissue—difficult to print and slow to dry—had been at first used, he now uses very thin tissue, so that the different thicknesses of gelatine which correspond to different tones are very minute. If we take the curve showing the relation between the distance of the microphone diaphragm from the magnet poles and the current strength at the receiver, it is found that only a short portion of such curve is suitable for the system, and much variation (and hence much thickness of film) is impossible in the position of his diaphragm. The microphone used is a large form of carbon instrument, in which the pressure of the diaphragm on three carbon balls varies their resistance, and therefore the strength of the current flowing through the circuit. With a large instrument of this type he can allow of much greater variation in the position of the diaphragm than is usual in the diaphragm of an ordinary telephone ; the latter, measured at the centre, being something like 10^{-6} cm. for a just audible sound.

By making use of a bridge arrangement, the balance of which is upset by the alteration in resistance of the carbon balls, Belin proposes to telegraph pictures over long distances with his modified appa-ratus, using a Blondel oscillograph of heavier type as regards field magnets, and a lighter suspension for the mirror. This could be turned through a greater angle for a given current if the wires to

Fig. 56.—Photograph transmitted by M. Belin's Telestereo-graph, over an artificial line.

which it was attached were increased in length and their tension lessened, but the period of swing would be greater.

M. Belin has obtained some good results with his system, an example of which is shown in Fig. 56. The results are, however, characterised by a soft diffused appearance, which is not always

a disadvantage. For the telegraphy of line drawings, pen-and-ink sketches, etc., he employs a
much simpler arrangement than the microphone,
a diagram of which is given in Fig. 57. A
metal arm FM is placed so that it can turn
about F, and it has a stylus S that presses lightly
against the transmitting drum. The line picture is prepared by the carbon process, and each
line is in high relief. When a line comes into con-

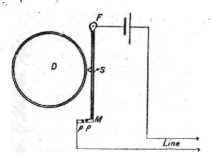

FIG. 57.

tact with the stylus the arm FM is pushed outwards, and the two platinums p, p are thrown out
of contact. This breaks the electric circuit, and
current no longer flows into the line to the receiver. It is claimed that this method is particularly
suitable for the transmission of writing or printed
matter, and might prove of value for international
banking purposes, etc. Such a transmitter is of
course only an alternative to the Casselli transmitter, as used in the Korn telautograph and the

author's telectrograph, and is not so practical, since the figure of merit of the contact breaker would require to be very high indeed to enable it to compete with the metal stylus tracing over a flush surface.

The synchronising arrangements, motors, etc., used in the telestereograph are so similar to those already described that any further reference to them is unnecessary. It may be said in conclusion, however, that M. Belin has found one solution to the problem of photo-telegraphy which may prove important when further matured.

CHAPTER VII.

THE TRANSMISSION OF PHOTOGRAPHS AND PICTURES BY WIRELESS TELEGRAPHY.

·ANY attempt to solve the somewhat delicate problem of transmitting photographs by " wireless " may at first sight seem unnecessary. But it remains to be seen whether, for long-distance work, it will not prove both more rapid and less expensive than transmission by cable, especially where much water intervenes as between America and Ireland or this country. As seen in Chapter V., the capacity of underground cables is very great as compared with ordinary overhead wires, besides which, between America and England, either two cables would be required, or one and an earth " return." The former would be extremely costly, and the latter would render necessary apparatus of a very delicate and sensitive character.

The prospects opened up by a wireless method. of transmission are, on the other hand, of an encouraging nature, as not only could long distances be covered at a high speed, but photographs of criminals could be telegraphed to ships fitted with a receiving apparatus, and sketches or plans could be transmitted between different sections of an army.

Mr. Hans Knudsen was the first to demonstrate a wireless apparatus, and I have since effected satisfactory transmissions by two new methods, which would be possible in actual practice over considerable distances, the latter method when developed being, in the opinion of some of our best wireless experts, capable of working across the Atlantic. The scheme of Knudsen would not, in my opinion, be practicable over any distance, for reasons that have been made clear by experiments carried out in my own wireless work.

Knudsen employed a flat plate on which a sketch in raised lines or a photograph in which the dark parts were resolved into lines in relief was placed. This travelled up under a style and back again, each upward travel being a fraction of an inch to the side of the previous one. A metal stylus was fixed over the flat plate, and this, by grazing against the raised parts of the picture, interrupted the primary of an induction coil, whose secondary was arranged with a spark gap. A coherer was used as the detector, and this was continuously decohered by a striker driven at a high speed by means of a small electro-motor ; the coherer actuated a relay which caused a pointed metal stylus to dig into the surface of a glass plate coated with lampblack ; an image of scratches was thus produced, which could be printed from like an ordinary photographic negative.

The synchronising was effected by the smoked glass plate throwing out the stylus circuit at each end of its travel and switching in another circuit which released it and set it free to travel again. The results were crude and streaky in appearance.

Mr. Knudsen gave some demonstrations in 1909 at the Hotel Cecil, and transmitted a picture of the King, by his wireless machines, across the room in which the apparatus was displayed.

Like most workers who begin their wireless studies on a modest scale, I used a coherer in the early experiments in order to detect the signals transmitted from the sending apparatus. These signals are of course regulated by the lines or dots of which the photographic image is composed, and the lines in a line drawing or half-tone photograph really act as the interruptors of the primary circuit.

It will be more convenient to describe briefly one or two of the ordinary methods of wireless tele-graphy, as the description of the photo-telegraphic apparatus will then be clearer to those whose work does not carry them into the "realm of wireless."

If we take an induction coil as shown in Fig. 58 and apply a suitable battery to the primary winding, the current of which can be rapidly interrupted by means of an interrupter I, a spark will pass between the terminals P, P of the secondary coil. If now we shunt these with a capacity K and an inductance X, and bring the spark balls P, P near together, the spark becomes very intense, and electrical oscillations are set up, the frequency of which is given by the expression

$$n = \frac{1}{2 \pi \sqrt{L C}},$$

where n is the frequency and L is the inductance

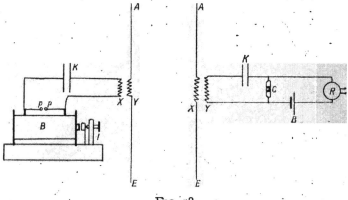

FIG. 58.

measured in centimetres, and C the capacity in microfarads.

If now we use the inductance X as the primary of a small transformer, and the secondary Y is placed between a connection to earth E and the aerial wire or wires of the antenna A, and the oscillation frequency of the aerial circuit tuned to that of the spark gap circuit, we have a transmitting station suitable for sending signals by wireless. If the current applied to the primary of the coil B can be interrupted by a Morse key, then by tapping for long and short periods we send out trains of damped waves for long and short periods respectively, which correspond to the dashes and dots used in the Morse code.

Now in wireless photo-telegraphy our transmitting machine clearly takes the part of the Morse key, and just as a sentence of words and letters can be made up of dots and dashes, so a photographic image is constructed of long or short marks in proper sequence on the receiving drum of the telectrograph.

In a simple receiving circuit we have the aerial antenna A and earth plate E connected with the ends of a coil X placed close to another coil Y of very fine wire, which latter transmits the wireless "oscillation" through a condenser K into the coherer C. A battery B and relay R are also in series with the coherer, which becomes conductive when the aerial receives an electro-magnetic-wave. The relay is thus actuated, and, by means of a local circuit closed by it, a small electro - magnetic hammer is made to tap the coherer, which then becomes non-conductive again, so that the relay contact is unmade.

An ordinary form of coherer is an exhausted glass tube, in the centre of which are two silver plugs near together, a part of the intermediate space being filled with silver and nickel filings. When a current is received these filings cohere and make tolerable contact, so that the wires connected to the silver plugs will convey a current. The cohesion requires then to be destroyed by a tap or knock, when the coherer again becomes a sensitive

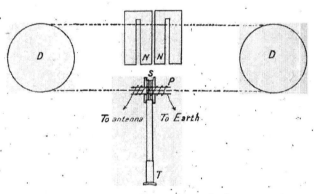

FIG. 59.—Diagram of Marconi's Electromagnetic Detector.

detector. A far more satisfactory arrangement devised by Marconi for detecting the signals is seen in Fig. 59. Here a string made of fine soft-iron wires travels round two discs D, D, which are actuated by clockwork. A glass tube fits over a small portion of the travelling wire, round which is wound a fine wire coil, the ends of this coil being connected to the antenna and earth plate respectively. A small secondary coil S wound over the

primary S goes to a sensitive telephone T. Two
horseshoe magnets are placed as shown in the
diagram, with similar poles together, and as the
wire string travels past them the magnetism induced
is retained by hysteresis, this being immediately
destroyed by the passing of the wireless oscillations through P, the magnetism shifting back

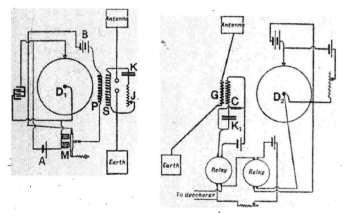

Fig. 60.—Arrangement first used by the Author for the
wireless transmission of pictures.

again to the normal position. This change of the
induced magnetism with respect to the magnets
causes a sound in the telephone, which is sufficiently sensitive to respond to currents of 10^{-13} ampère
and less.

The first wireless pictures transmitted with any
success—and I am speaking of success from an
experimental point of view—were obtained with the

apparatus shown diagrammatically in Fig. 60. The left-hand side shows the transmitter, the right the receiving arrangement.

D is the drum of a telectrograph as described in Chapter IV., the stylus tracing over a sketch drawn in insulating ink on a sheet of lead foil ; D and the style had a condenser shunted across to prevent sparking. The current from the battery A was interrupted by the lines of the picture, the magnetism in M being thus intermittent. The relay at M broke the contact of the battery B in circuit with the primary P of an induction coil, S being the secondary, electrical oscillations being set up in the manner already described.

A negative print was used on the drum D, so that sparking between the balls took place only when a " line " in the picture was in contact with the stylus. The capacity K and inductance J in the oscillatory circuit could be adjusted, and for long distances the aerial and earth would be connected inductively.

A short wave of about 40 metres was employed, this being determined by the expression

$$\frac{v}{\lambda} = \frac{5 \times 10^6}{\sqrt{\text{capacity inductance}}},$$

where $v = 3 \times 10^{10}$ cm. $=$ the velocity of electro-magnetic oscillations, and λ is the wave-length.

Turning now to the receiving circuit the aerial and earth were connected to the primary of a " jigger," the current being transformed down by the secondary, and passed through the coherer with a condenser K in series. A rather insensitive relay

FIG. 61.—Sketch of head and shoulders of a lady. Transmitted by wireless.

of the telephone service pattern was inserted in the coherer-battery circuit, the battery consisting of two dry cells. The local circuit of this relay actuated a second relay through another battery of two dry cells, and the local circuit of this second relay included the receiving circuit of the telectrograph, as shown in the diagram.

The use of a contrary current running through the receiver was necessary to render the marks clear and short.

A local shunt circuit was also used from the first relay to actuate the decoherer, which consisted of a

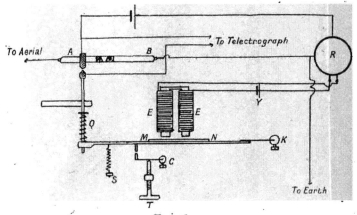

FIG. 62.

very lightly built electro-magnetic striker which tapped the coherer. This decohesion was later effected in a much simpler manner, the act of striking the coherer closing a local circuit which produced an electrolytic mark on the paper of the receiving drum.

In the figure, EE is an electro-magnet, the windings in series with the battery Y, and the local side of the relay R. The coherer AB was fixed in rigid supports, and to one end was attached a fixed brass collar fitted with a platinum pin P, the magnet armature MN consisted of a piece of iron tape fitted to an aluminium rod ending in a piece of spring brass fixed to the pillar K. The striker was fitted to the end of this light rod and when it struck, the force of the blow was taken off owing to its ability to work back through a hole in the rod, the spring Q keeping it normally in a fixed position. When the platinum pins touched, the force of impact decohered the coherer, and also completed the circuit of the electrolytic receiver. In this way I was able to get a very precise movement, in which one short wave train caused one tap ; hence one mark was made on the telectrograph paper for one dot or " contact " in the transmitter.

· The " stickiness " of coherers, however, renders good synchronising difficult, and a straight line would always appear somewhat wavy in the received picture. Moreover, if the apparatus were working with certainty, rapidity was impossible, and after making various interesting records, the work was continued on other lines.

I will now proceed to describe the most recent wireless methods which promise to give more satisfactory results, especially as original experiments make it probable that half-tone photographs will be transmitted at a considerable speed with the apparatus:*

The transmitting apparatus consists, as before, of a metal drum revolving under a stylus, a metal foil print, the image of which consists of glue or shellac lines, being wrapped round it. The battery

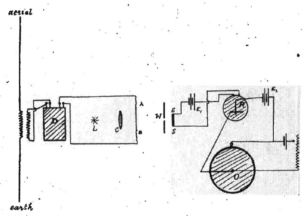

FIG. 63.—Quartz string and selenium cell arranged for receiving and transforming up electrical oscillations.

current flows through the cylinder, picture, and stylus to a very lightly-built relay capable of working at a high speed ; this relay in turn actuates a heavier one which causes the interruptions in the primary of the alternator or induction coil. If a coil be used, a turbine or other mercury brake is essential.

* Prov. Patent 361/10.

The oscillations are transformed at the receiving station and the secondary of the transformer is connected to a valve receiver (Marconi), this in turn being connected with a battery E and the

FIG. 64.—Sketch of the King transmitted by the Author's wireless apparatus.

string AB of a large galvanometer. The construction of the galvanometer is somewhat similar to that of Korn's modification of the Einthoven instrument, already described at some length. The " string " AB is in this case, however, a quartz fibre, silvered, about $\frac{1}{12000}$th inch in diameter. It is free to move laterally in a very powerful magnetic field, and a current of 10^{-8} ampères will displace it to a considerable extent.

Light from a powerful but steady arc L passes through the condensing lens C so as to form a shadow of the wire AB upon a fine metal slit H. When a current passes through the wire and causes it to shift, the slit is uncovered, and light passes through and illuminates a very sensitive selenium cell SS. A weak current passes through this cell from the battery E_1 into a sensitive relay R, which also has a high speed of working. When the selenium cell is feebly illuminated, its resistance drops, and the current is sufficiently increased to actuate the relay. The local circuit of the relay includes a battery of about 20 volts and the telectrograph receiver Q, a contrary current being passed through a resistance into it also, as a shunt in the manner indicated in the diagram.

As the image is visible, being received by the electrolytic method, it is not necessary to have any synchronising gear on the receiver. A datum line is drawn right across the picture being transmitted, and near the commencement. The reproduction of this line is carefully watched during the reception, and the line is made to lie close against a line drawn across the electrolytic paper. If the line being received diverges from the drawn line then it is known that the receiving drum is travelling either too quickly or too slowly, and the motor is regulated accordingly.

It will be seen that the wireless transmission of pictures requires both delicate adjustment, and accurately-built driving machinery. We are depending on a movement of about the five-thousandth part of an inch for our recording, and there are a number of pieces of delicate apparatus, all reciprocative, which require to be in perfect harmony.

In all such work as this results can only be obtained slowly, and progress is often only apparent to those actually in touch with it. Time alone will show to what extent wireless photo-telegraphy will be of value.

INDEX

P.T.

L.

Lightning Source UK Ltd.
Milton Keynes UK
UKHW050147070223
416537UK00019B/2706